LORETTA SANTINI

ROME AND VATICAN

Published and printed by

Narni - Terni 1993
ITALIA

D1219482

INDEX

INTRODUCTION

This Guide has been compiled by the Publishers with the idea of giving the reader a great deal of brief information, which will enable him above all to find his way about among the manifold beauties of the City of Rome.

It remains for the reader himself to select from among them those best suited to his taste and to the time at his disposal.

Preference has therefore been given to describing places and works of art, without listing them in too much detail, so as to come to the essentials immediately, that is to say, to what is indispensable for giving a comprehensive picture of an itinerary, a style, a work of art or an artist.

Only the most famous and important of the many thousands of works of art preserved in Museums and Galleries have been mentioned, but this has been done in such a way as to enable everyone to realise the importance of the Museum or work of art in question.

Thus the Guide is handy and clear for everyone who wants to become acquainted with Rome in its true and most personal aspect, and for all those lovers of art who are looking for the finest works and for the city's local colour.

It might further be added that it seems superfluous to talk about Rome in general, its fascination, history and countless traditions: indeed, Rome speaks for herself, and there is nothing to be added to the impressions of those who walk along her streets, who are acquainted with her long history, who love her sunsets and recognise the imprint of art in every corner.

So nothing remains to be done but to throw a coin in the Trevi Fountain in order to ensure our return.

L. S.

Our visit to this beautiful City starts at Piazza Venezia, its ideal and, one might also say, its geographical centre, since it will be the starting point for all the itineraries in seach of the manifold and picturesque attractions of Rome and of its long and interesting history.

As has already been said, PIAZZA VENEZIA may be considered the centre of Rome. The square is not only the fulcrum of its political, religious and social life, but also a point of reference for the visitor, It is from here that the most important thoroughfares of the city radiate: Via IV Novembre, leading to Via Nazionale, and then on to Piazza Esedra and the Railway Station (Stazione Termini): Via del Plebiscito, which, by way of Corso Vittorio Emmanuele, leads to St. Peter's; Via del Corso, which runs to Piazza Colonna and Piazza del Popolo; Via dei Fori Imperiali, which crosses the main centre of ancient Rome.

It is a regular square, dominated by the spectacular Monument to Victor Emmanuel II.

The square derives its name from Palazzo Venezia.

MONUMENT TO
VICTOR EMMANUEL II

PALAZZO VENEZIA

PALAZZO VENEZIA

This was built in 1455 by Cardinal Pietro Barbo, who later became Pope Paul II. It is one of the finest examples of Renaissance architecture. It is sometimes attributed to **Rossellino,** at other times to the architect **Leon Battista Alberti.** In any case, it is an austere, imposing but, on the whole, harmonious building, articulated by a row of fine windows (note particularly those of the central fascia with the Guelf cross).

At first the palace was a Papal residence, and later became the seat of the Venetian Embassy, from which it took its name. In 1797 it passed to the Austrian Embassy, until, after being handed back to Italy, it became the seat of the Fascist Government.

It was reopened to the public in 1943, immediately after the fall of Fascism, and now houses a MUSEUM as well as important art exhibitions.

To the left of Palazzo Venezia stands the

ST. MARK'S BASILICA

built in the 4th century A.D. and altered several times, especially in the 15th century. The façade and portico are probably the work of **L. B. Alberti.** The interior is richly decorated in the baroque style, with a fine Renaissance coffered ceiling. The mosaics in the apse are of earlier origin (11th century). In the Basilica there are also works by **Canova, Melozzo da Forlì** and **Mino da Fiesole.**

In a corner of the little square of San Marco there is a bust of Isis, known by the name of "Madama Lucrezia". This is one of the many "talking statues" of Rome, that is to say, statues to which popular imagination attributes the power to speak and to pass judgments on the habits and various events of the times, thus becoming a vehicle for the satire of the lively Roman people.

We now take a look at the imposing, well known MONUMENT TO VICTOR EMMANUEL II erected to celebrate the 50th anniversary of the Kingdom of Italy to the design of the architect **G. Sacconi,** and also known as the **"Vittoriano".** It commemorates the unity of Italy and therefore symbolises the

THE CAPITOL

Fatherland, Military Valour, the Risorgimento and the Nation. Thus it is looked upon as the Altar of the Fatherland, for the Monument also contains the body of the ''Unknown Soldier''; that is to say the body of a nameless soldier who fell in battle during the 1915-18 war. The most important ceremonies to commemorate historic anniversaries are held in front of the body of this unknown warrior, symbol of the sacrifice of so many Italian soldiers.

The Monument is decorated with a great number of sculptures. The equestrian statue of **Victor Emmanuel II** to whom the Monument is dedicated, dominates all the rest. It is by the sculptor **Chiaradia.** On its plinth are represented the towns of Italy which helped towards the nation's unification (by **Maccagnini).** The great staircase with its several flights leads to the Altar of the Fatherland, a work by **Zanelli,** culminating in the statue symbolising Rome.

On its right is the allegory of ''Patriotism triumphant'', on the left ''The Triumph of Labour''. The fountains on either side of the staircase represent the Adriatic and the Tyrrhenian Sea, and above them are other statues symbolising Law, Sacrifice, Harmony and Might. On the left of the Monument are the remains of the tomb of **C. Publicius Bibulus** (1st century B.C.).

Above the colonnade are statues representing the regions of Italy. The two chariots on top of the Propylaeum represent Liberty and the Unity of Italy. Inside the building are housed the Library, the Archives, and the Museum and Institute for the History of the Italian Risorgimento.

THE CAPITOL

is the spiritual centre of Rome, just as it was the religious centre of ancient Rome. It stands on a low hill, the Capitoline (one of the seven hills on which the city is built), and its terraces command a vast panorama with a view of the remains of ancient Rome and the buildings of medieval and modern Rome in a wide sweep.

The Capitoline Hill, seized by the Romans from the

THE CAPITOL

CAPITOLIAN MUSEUMS - Capitoline She-Wolf

Sabines, was the scene of the most important historical events which were the glory of ancient Rome. On its two crests stand the **Arx Capitolina** (at present the site of the **Church of Aracoeli**), which was a rock dedicated to June, and the **Temple of Jupiter Optimus Maxims** (the remains of which can be seen in the Museum in the Palazzo dei Conservatori). Between the two summits, in the hollow which is now the Piazza del Campidoglio, there was in ancient times the "Asylum", that is to say the place made accessible to the plebs by Romulus, the first King of Rome, so that they might dwell there in safety.

In the course of the centuries, the hill underwent various transformations and alterations, until it took on its present aspect which is mainly the result of Michelangelo's plan.

The PIAZZA DEL CAMPIDOGLIO has on its three sides the **Senator's Palace** (in the centre), the **Palazzo dei Conservatori** (on the right), and the **Palazzo dei Musei** (on the left). It is reached from Piazza Venezia, leaving on the left the Victor Emmanuel Monument and the remains of an ancient Roman house, and then ascending the central ramp from Via del Teatro Marcello.

This great ramp, leading up to the Piazza, was designed by Michelangelo, like all the rest of the square, to the commission of Pope Paul III. On the way up, there is on the left the Monument to **Cola di Rienzo** by **Masini** (1887), commemorating the sacrifice of this son of the people who paid with his life for his dream of restorating to Rome the glory and might of the Republican period. Nearby, in a cage, is kept a she-wolf, symbol of Rome.

At the top of the ramp leading to the Capitol, there are, on either side, the statues of the **Dioscuri, Castor and Pollux**, with their horses, together with other statues, including that of **Constantine** and the so-called **Trophies of Marius,** i.e. the trophies of arms taken from the Barbarians.

The whole square and the buildings surrounding it were architecturally arranged by **Michelangelo** between 1546 and 1550.

He partially transformed the already existing **Senator's Place**, connecting it with the square by means of a large staircase (in part altered and reduced in the

CAPITOLIAN MUSEUMS - Hall Orazi and Curiazi

execution). He then built the two palaces at the sides (the **Palazzo dei Conservatori** and the **Palazzo dei Musei**), enlivening their façades with a powerful order of pilasters, and making them diverge slightly towards the centre in order to bring the palace in the blackground seemingly nearer.

The geometric pattern on the pavement of the square, conceived in the form of expanding and crossing elliptical shapes was also designed by him, and harmonises well with the architecture of the whole. In 1535 Michelangelo took **the statue of Marcus Aurelius** from the Lateran and set it up in the centre of the square; it is the sole remaining example of the equestrian statues of the Roman imperial period. There are various theories and legends to explain the reasons which made it possible for this monument to come down to us. The main reason, however, is to be found in the fact that it was long thought to represent the Emperor Constantine, the first to allow the practice of the Christian religion.

In the space created by the divergence of the stairs leading to the Senator's Palace, Michelangelo had a fountain placed with statues representing the **Goddess of Rome** in the centre, and the **Nile** and **Tiber** on either side. The statue of **Rome Triumphant** was originally a statue of Minerva, but Pope Sixtus V, who during his pontificate had started a vigorous campaign to revitalise Christianity, threatened to have the Capitol demolished, unless all the statues dedicated to pagan deities were removed. Nevertheless he agreed to have this statue transformed into that of Rome Triumphant, after the goddess's sword had been replaced by a cross.

The SENATOR'S PALACE: This is at present the official seat of Mayor of Rome. It was built over the ancient Tabularium, erected in the time of the Republic to house all the laws written on "tabulae" (whence the name).

The Senator's Palace was built on it in the 13th century (the visit to the Tabularium will be described later).

Above the Senator's Palace rises the 16th century **Capitoline Tower**: it still contains the **Patarine Bell** which has been rung for many centuries only on particularly important occasions, such as, for instance, the anniversary of the foundation of Rome (April 21). At the top of the tower a cross was placed as the symbol of the Christianity of Rome.

The interior of the Senator's Palace contains many rooms, of which the most important are: the **Hall of the Municipal Council**, also called the Hall of **Julius Caesar** because of a statue of **Caesar**, dating from 150 A.D.; **the Hall of the Banners**; the **Hall of the Municipal Committee**; the **Hall of Cleopatra** (from the statue of that name).

THE PALACE OF THE CAPITOLINE MUSEUM: this is to the left of the Senator's Palace. It is so called because it contains a rich and interesting Museum of classical art. The most important works are:

In the courtyard: statue of **Marforio**, one of the "talking statues" of Rome, the interlocutor of "Pasquino", another of the talking statues, with whom — according to the legend — he carries on lively satirical dialogues, hence known as "Pasquinades".

A corridor leads to the various rooms; in it there are several statues of Roman times, including **Diana the Huntress** and a **Minerva**.

The three ground floor rooms contain fragments of bas-reliefs, outstanding among them the **sarcophagus of Alexander Severus**.

A staircase leads to the upper floor with other interesting rooms.

Room 1: it contains the famous **Dying Gaul**, a copy of a magnificent Greek sculpture. It dates from about 200 B.C. and was found in the Gardens of Sallust. Its fine modelling and remarkable expression make it a splendid example of ancient art.

Room 2: various busts, inscriptions and fragments.

Room 3: this room contains a series of very interesting statues, among them a fine pair of **Centaurs**.

Room 4: this is called **the Room of the Philosophers**, because it contains the busts of men outstanding in the history of thought, in addition to the so-called "seated figure", probably a portrait of **M. Claudius Marcellus**, the Roman general who took Syracuse after a siege during the Second Punic War.

Room 5: it contains the busts of many Roman emperors and affords a veritable survey of Roman portraiture of the imperial period.

Cabinet of the Capitoline Venus: it takes its name from the so-called **Capitoline Venus**, a very fine copy of a Greek original of the fourth century B.C.

Room of the Doves: so-called after the **lovely mosaic of doves**, a fine example of Alexandrian art, found at Hadrian's Villa.

The PALAZZO DEI CONSERVATORI: to the right of the Senator's Palace. It contains a great number of works of art in a series of rooms and galleries as follows: **Room of the Conservatori — Museum of the Conservatori** (with its Old and New Sections) — the **Capitoline Picture Gallery**.

The Palace was built by **Della Porta** and **Longhi il Vecchio** to the design of **Michelangelo**.

Room of the Conservatori: it is reached by way of a courtyard with a portico containing various archaeological finds.

Room I: known as the Room of the **Horatii and Curiatii** after the frescoes by Cesari (the Cavalier d'Ar-

pino). There are some interesting statues of **Popes by Bernini** and **Algardi**.

Room II: this contains the statues of the **Pontifical Captains**.

Room III: here is the marvellous **Boy with the Thorn**, a copy of a very fine Greek original of the fifth century B.C.

Room IV: this contains the **Capitoline She-wolf**, the symbol of Rome: it is an Etruscan work, to which the twins were later added to represent Romulus and Remus.

In **Rooms V to X** there are many other works of art, as well as **Roman and Flemish 18th century tapestries**.

The next rooms form a part of the MUSEO DEI CONSERVATORI: this also contains sculptures of considerable artistic value, including the statue of the **Charioteer** (copy of a Greek original of the fifth century); there is also an important collection of **Attic and Corinthian vases**, as well as **Etruscan bronzes** and **sarcophagi**.

In recent times, a new series of rooms has been arranged on the site of the **Temple of Jupiter Capitolinus**, containing Roman works of the Republican period as well as portraits, sarcophagi and so on.

We now come to the CAPITOLINE PICTURE GALLERY: the collection was arranged by Pope Benedict XIV, but was later enlarged and rearranged with the aim of leaving in it only the most valuable and original works. Among the masterpieces are some portraits by **Van Dyck**, and a magnificent **Velasquez**; there are also works by **Dosso Dossi, Tintoretto, Veronese, Parmigianino, Guercino**, and many others.

Important also the china collection in the Corridor "delle Porcellane".

By way of Via del Campidoglio, which runs along the right of the Senator's Palace, the **Temple of Vejovis** is reached.

The Senator's Palace, which, as already mentioned, was built over the **Tabularium**, is irregular, almost trapezoidal, in form, because one side is shortened by the site of the above mentioned Temple. Lower down, on the outside of the Tabularium, is a terrace which overlooks the Roman Forum below. The political and religious life of ancient Rome centred upon the valley which stretches between the Capitoline and the Palatine on one side, and towards the Quirinal on the other; here arose the Roman civilisation that was to spread later to the very ends of the then known world.

Going up again by the road on the right which crosses Via del Monte Tarpeo, one notes the remains of the **Temple of Jupiter**; proceeding then to the Belvedere which dominates the **Tarpeian Rock**. Originally the Capitoline Hill was called the Tarpeian after this rock, of ill fame in ancient times, because it was from here that all those who had betrayed the nation were hurled down to their death. (The custom had its origin in the legend of the young girl Tarpeia who betrayed the Romans by opening the gates to the Sabines).

CAPITOLIAN MUSEUMS ⋏
Persian Sibyl

CAPITOLIAN MUSEUMS
St. John Baptist   ⋎

CAPITOLIAN MUSEUMS ⋏
Picture of Young Lady

CAPITOLIAN MUSEUMS
Shepherd Matius   ⋎

THE CHURCH OF S. MARIA IN ARACOELI

VIA DEI FORI IMPERIALI ➤

THE CHURCH OF S. MARIA IN ARACOELI

stands on the Capitoline rock, and is reached by climbing the long staircase to the right of the Capitoline Museum, or by way of the stairs built by the Romans on the initiative of Cola di Rienzo in 1348 as a votive offering for having escaped the perilous plague.

The Church, which was built around the sixth century, played a very important part in the life of Rome, especially in medieval times, when it was loocked upon as the centre of the religious and social life of Rome, and frequented by the nobility and the most famous people of the period, who, often gathered there to deliberate on weighty questions concerning the life of the community. The Church was from time to time entrusted to various monastic orders, until it was assigned to the Franciscan Friars by Pope Innocent IV (1250). In addition to its importance for religious life and social and art history, the Church is famous for the **Bambino d'Aracoeli**, a wooden statue of the Child Jesus, carved out of olive wood from the Garden of Gethsemane.

The statue, which dates from the seventh century, is displayed in the crib every year at the Christmas season. It is also thought to possess miraculous powers, and it is traditional today for children to go and recite Christmas poems in front of it. The Bambino, when not displayed in the crib, is kept in the Sacristy Chapel.

The Church, which appears from the outside as a huge mass of masonry, indicating the three aisles inside only by the different levels of its parts, is richly decorated inside with art treasures of various periods,

Above all, the fine 12th century Cosmatic pavement with its marble inlays should be noted. The ceiling dates from the 16th century, and commemorates by its symbols the naval battle of Lepanto, which represented the joint victory of the maritime republics (in particular

of Venice) over the pirates, and the victory of Christianity over the enemies of the Faith.

Right Aisle: just at the side of the main entrance is the **Tomb of Cardinal d'Albret** of Bregno (15th century) and a tombstone by **Donatello**.

First Chapel: frescoes by Pinturicchio, depicting the Life of S. Bernardino.

Second Chapel: this contains a **Pietà** by **Marco da Siena**.

Chapels III to VIII contain works of the 17th and 19th centuries.

Ninth Chapel: here is the fine **Tomb of Honorius IV** and that of **Enrico Savelli**, both in Cosmatic technique (13th century).

In one of the Transept chapels is a 13th century mosaic of S. Rosa.

Presbytery: on the High Altar, the **Madonna of Aracoeli**.

In the left transept, the Chapel of St. Helena with an urn containing her remains. In the same chapel is the **Tomb of Cardinal Matteo d'Acquasparta** (a General of the Franciscans. In the Divine Comedy, Dante mentions him as being responsible for the decline of the order).

The tomb is perhaps the work of **Giovanni di Cosma** (14th century), and the fresco above is by **Cavallini** or one of his pupils.

Left Aisle

Of particular interest, the Second Chapel, where the crib is placed every year and the statue of the Child Jesus, referred to above, is displayed.

The other chapels of the left aisle contain various works of art from different centuries, among them two **13th century pulpits** by the **Cosmati** brothers.

14

THE ROMAN FORUM

May be reached from the Capitol by going down to the right of the Senator's Palace, or by skirting the Victor Emmanuel Monument and taking Via dei Fori Imperiali.

The term Roman Forum is used to indicate the place assigned in ancient Rome for the meetings of the people; here public, and above all private business was contracted, public debates were held, and here too, justice was meted out by the great Roman lawyers, appropriately called forensic.

The Forum was the city's most important political and social centre; it was the very cradle of Roman civilisation which gave its orders and instruction to all the peoples it subjected.

Originally the area where the Roman Forum was built, was swampy and unhealthy owing to the stagnation of the waters flowing into it from the **Cloaca Maxima**. After the place had been drained, it became the site of trade between the Romans and the inhabitants of the surroundings areas. As the city's life became established, the place gradually took on the character of an organised centre, and at that time the "tavernae" (today called shops) and temples were built. Thus it slowly lost its use as a market place and became the centre of political and juridical life, as previously mentioned.

Owing to the steady development and growth of Rome and its increasing importance on the social, commercial and especially the political plane, the Roman Forum soon became too small, and thus, especially in the Republican period, other Fora were established, that is to say, other meeting places, consisting of large areas or squares, surrounded by important public buildings, and generally comprising also a temple or a building commemorating some noteworthy historical event.

Thus it was that the construction of the Roman Forum was followed by that of the **Imperial Fora**, **Trajan's Forum** (to commemorate the Dacian wars), the **Forum of Augustus** (to commemorate the Battle of Philippi), the **Fora of Caesar**, **Vespasian** and **Domitian**.

MAMERTINE PRISON

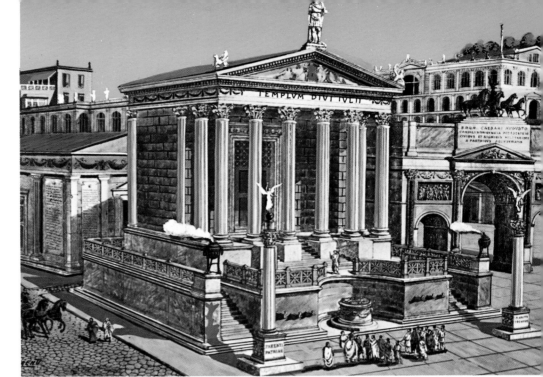

ROMAN FORUM
Reconstruction

ROMAN FORUM

The Roman Forum suttered considerable damage from the Barbarian invasions, in addition to that from losses due to plundering by fanatic lovers of antiquities. A great deal of material was also carried off for use in fortifications or the construction of new buildings, so much so that it soon fell into a state of complete neglect and was used for assembling cattle (whence it is still known by the name of "Campo Vaccino"). In the 18th century excavations were started again, which brought to light remarkable artistic treasures, although in sadly damaged condition.

Now for a visit to the Roman Forum.

All along its length runs the **Via Sacra** which led right up to the Capitol, and which still partly preserves its original paving.

On the Via del Foro Romano we first come to the **Porticus Deorum Consentium**, built in 367 A.D. (hence, one of the last temples dedicated to the mosto important pagan gods); now only nine columns of it remain.

Next follows the **Temple of Vespasian** commissioned by the Emperor Domitian; three fine columns with Corinthian capitals remain, then the **Temple of Concord**, built to commemorate the agreement reached between Patricians and Plebs after the last of innumerable struggles on the part of the Plebs to gain equal rights; the temple was rebuilt in Imperial times by Tiberius. Today only the base that supported it remains.

ROMAN FORUM
1 - The Temple of Saturne
2 - Via Sacra
3 - The Temple of Vespasianus
4 - The Rostrums
5 - The Arch of Septimius Severus
6 - The Curia
7 - Basilica Emilia
8 - The Basilica of Maxentius
9 - The Temple of Antonius and Faustina
10 - The Colosseum
11 - The Round Temple of Romulus

12 - The Column of Foca
13 - The Temple of Julius Caesar
14 - The Temple of Venus and Rome
15 - The Arch of Titus
16 - Temple of Vesta
17 - The House of the Vestal Virgins
18 - The Temple of Castor and Pollux
19 - The Church of Santa Maria Antigua
20 - The Palatine Hill
21 - The Temple of Augustus
22 - Basilica Giulia

FORO ROMANO - RICOSTRUZIONE

ROMAN FORUM
Reconstruction

1 - The Curia
2 - The Arch of Septimius Severus
3 - Basilica Emilia
4 - Basilica of Maxentius
5 - The Temple of Antoninus and Faustina

6 - The Colosseum
7 - The Round Temple of Romulus
8 - The Temple of Venus and Rome
9 - The Temple of Julius Caesar
10 - The Arch of Titus

11 - The House of the Vestals
12 - The Church of Santa Maria Antiqua
13 - The Palatine Hill
14 - The Temple of Augustus
15 - Temple of Vesta

16 - The Temple of Castor and Pollux
17 - Basilica Julia
18 - The Column of Foca
19 - The Rostrums
20 - Via Sacra

21 - The Temple of Saturn

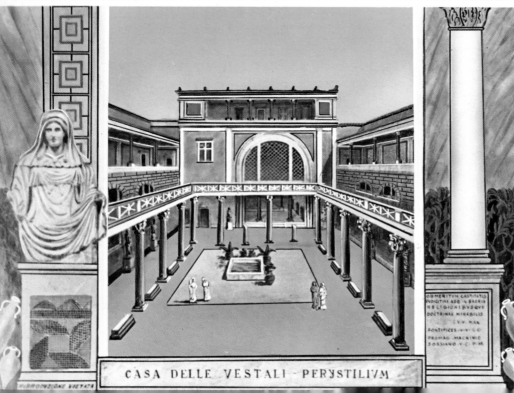

CASA DELLE VESTALI · PERYSTILIVM

ROMAN FORUM
House of Vestals

ROMAN FORUM
House of Vestals
(Reconstruction)

ROMAN FORUM

ROMAN FORUM
Reconstruction

25

THE ARCH OF SEPTIMIUS SEVERUS

THE ARCH OF TITUS ➤

In a wide place stands the **Church of St. Joseph of the Carpenters**, dating from 1540, and built over the remains of the ill-famed **Mamertine Prison.** This ancient construction consists of two cells: one is the real Mamertine Prison, the ancient Roman prison where famous historical personalities met with their death. The second cell is also called the **Tullianum**, perhaps because it was built by **Servius Tullius.** Probably the place was originally a large well, and was later used as a prison for criminals and prisoners of war condemned to death. St. Peter may also have been imprisoned here; according to tradition, he performed the miracle of making water gush from the rock to quench the thirst of the other prisoners and to baptise many of his fellow prisoners, whom, together with two jailers, he had converted to Christianity. On this account, the place was revered in the Middle Ages, and was given the name of **S. Pietro in Carcere.**

On the opposite side stands the Church of the **Saints Luke and Martina.**

It consists of two churches, built in the 8th century and rebuilt in the 18th. One of the artists was **Pietro da Cortona** (1634), who worked mainly on the façade and the high altar of the upper Church. The church contains the tombs of many painters and sculptors.

The lower Church, which is particularly interesting, was built out of remains of the previous buildings which were connected with the Roman Curia.

The Curia, which was the ancient meeting place of the Roman Senate, is near by, as one goes towards the Basilica Aemilia. It was founded by Tullius Hostilius and rebuilt several times: in 638, it was turned into a church, and has been remodelled several times. Modern restorations have given back to the Curia its original appearance. In particular, the ancient meeting hall has been restored, faced with marble, with the platforms where the seats of the Roman senators were set out.

Beyond the Curia are the remains of the **Basilica Aemilia**, to the right of the main entrance to the Roman Forum, the one opening on Via dei Fori Imperiali. **M. Aemilius Lepidus and M. Fulvius Nobilior** had the Basilica built in 179 A.D. It was damaged and restored several times. It was originally 100 metres long, and

26

was surrounded by a large colonnade. It still bears traces of the fire which destroyed it, together with a large part of the Forum.

The origin of the Roman Basilica is uncertain, but probably it derives from the typical Greek portico. At Rome, the basilica was put to particular uses: it was a place where justice was administered, and also a meeting place for making business deals. The Roman basilica was destined to figure largely in art owing to its architecture: in fact, it is from this type of building that the future Christian basilica was to take its name and also the ground plan in its essential features.

Continuing our visit to the Forum, we note the space in front of the Curia: this was the **Comitium**, where the assemblies of the people were held, which gave Rome a system of justice and wise administration.

Opposite the Comitium, a piece of roofing covers the famous **Lapis Niger**, renowned for two things: in the first place, there is on the large slab of dark stone an inscription which is the most ancient Latin text yet known (6th century); in addition, beneath the stone, there is a tomb which is probably that of Romulus. The great importance attributed to this monument in antiquity makes this fairly certain.

Let us now take a look at the great **Arch of Septimius Severus**, still virtually intact. It was erected in the third century A.D. to celebrate the victories won by Septimius Severus over the Parthians. It is a fine triple arch, its three openings being separated by white grooved columns resting on high plinths. Beyond the Arch of Septimius Severus, a round base (the so-called **Umbilicus Urbis**), indicates the centre of the ancient city. On its left is the **Rostra**, or platform, from which Roman orators delivered their speeches; the platform only remains. The Rostra extends towards the square of the Forum, which is dominated by the **Column of Phocas** (an emperor in the 7th century A.D.). Nearby are the **Screens (Plutei) of Trajan**, two large carved transennae, which previously formed the parapets of the tribune of the Rostra. On the inner side of one are pictures of animals — a pig, a ram and a bull to be sacrificed to the gods; on the other is represented a fiscal amnesty granted to the debtor cities, since the state treasury was filled with the proceeds from victorious wars. On the other side of the plutei are commemorated in sculpture the most glorious events of Trajan's reign.

The **Via Sacra**, already mentioned before, passes not far from the ruins of Temple of Diocletian; it derives its name from the fact that Romulus and Titus Tatius passed along it after having stipulated a pact of friendship, and also because it was the road taken by the priests during religious ceremonies. At first it led from the Palatine to the Temple of Vesta; it was later extended as far as the Capitol, so that it passed through the whole Roman Forum.

Beyond the Via Sacra is the **Basilica Julia**, built at the order of Caesar to celebrate the Julian family. The **Temple of Saturn** is seen next; it was built in the Republican period about the sixth century B.C., and is therefore one of the oldest temples. Here was the public treasury, of which a few columns still remain. The three fine Corinthian columns on the other side of the Basilica Julia form part of the **Temple of Castor and Pollux**, or Temple of the Dioscuri. Further along the Via Sacra, on the right, stands the **Temple of Julius Caesar**, the **Arch of Augustus**, the **Spring of Juturna** (where according to legend, the Dioscuri watered their horses), the **Oratory of the Forty Martyrs**, with the remains of eighth century frescoes, and the **Church of Santa Maria Antiqua**, made out of a pagan building and especially interesting on account of the frescoes from various periods that decorate it, as well as for the particular ground plan of the building. Now, on the right of the church, is the **Temple of Augustus**, part of which is incorporated with the Church of Santa Maria Antiqua.

Going back to the Arch of Augustus, the foundations of the **Regia**, should be noted, the residence of the first kings and the seat of the State Archives, containing the Annals, that is to say, the books into which were transcribed the principal events of the city's history. Opposite the Regia stands the **Temple of Vesta**, circular in shape; it was founded by Numa Pompilius to symbolise the continuity of the life of Rome; inside it, burned perpetually the sacred fire, symbol of the unquenchable life of the State. For this reason it was particularly important to keep this fire always alight, and hence the order of the Vestal Virgins was created to tend the flame continuosly. These Virgins dwelt in the **House of the Vestals** nearby.

Still on the Via Sacra, one comes to the **Temple of Antonius and Faustina**, dedicated to the Emperor Antoninus Pius and his wife. The Temple was later made into a church which took the name of the **Church of San Lorenzo in Miranda**. The two buildings are today partly merged, so that in front of the 17th century façade, there stand the beautiful and elegant columns of the Temple.

On the right of the Temple, an **ancient Necropolis** has been discovered; the material found there has been transferred to the Museum of the Forum. Further along the Via Sacra there is, on the left, another circular **Temple**, which proved difficult to identify. It has a fine bronze door, with the original lock.

The little temple serves as the Vestibule of a square building, known in the 17th century as the **Templum Sacrae Urbis**, and later transformed into the **Church of SS. Cosma and Damian** (of which more later on).

Next on the left of the Via Sacra, are seen the remains of the **Basilica of Maxentius**, a grand building, which will be described more fully when it is reached by the Via dei Fori Imperiali, together with the **Church of Santa Francesca Romana.**

The Via Sacra ends near the **Arch of Titus**, erected in honour of the Emperor Titus to commemorate the conquest of Jerusalem. The many bas-reliefs on it portray episodes of the victory and the triumph of Titus.

The Arch of Titus has a single opening, flanked by grooved and trabested half-columns.

BASILICA OF MAXENTIUS

BASILICA OF MAXENTIUS
(Reconstruction)

29

From Piazza Venezia one takes the road on the left, Via dei Fori Imperiali, a new street the construction of which brought once more to the light of day the various Fora that lie around it and from which it derives its name.

The Piazza del Foro Traiano is first reached, where stands the **Church of Santa Maria di Loreto**, a Renaissance building, partly the work of Sangallo, and the 18th century **Church of the Sacred Name of Maria.**

The Forum of Trajan, the remains of which can be seen, was built by Apollodorus of Damascus to the order of the Emperor Ulpius Trajanus to celebrate his victories over the Dacians. It was the last of the imperial fora to be built, and is certainly imposing with its superb architectural design. It was planned as a square, access to which was gained by a triumphal arch: it was surrounded by large colonnades, and in the centre stood the equestrian statue of the Emperor to whom it was dedicated. The **Basilica Ulpia** with its five naves covered a large area: to make room for it, Trajan had the high, uneven ground dug out to a depth equal to that of Trajan's Column. The four rows of columns of the central part of this Basilica still remain.

Trajan's Column was erected to immortalise the Emperor's achievements. It is 42 metres high. In its base there is a recess in which the Emperor's ashes were placed. On the top there has stood since the 16th century a statue of St. Peter, replacing that of Trajan, in accordance with the dispositions of the Church at that time.

Around the whole column runs a spiral frieze in bas-relief, illustrating the Dacian wars as well as the Emperor's activities in time of peace.

In addition to these buildings and monuments, and two libraries which have disappeared, there was also the **Temple of the Divine Trajan**, and, on the right of the Forum, still partly visible, **Trajan's Market**, which affords us one of the finest and most important examples of the Roman conception of space, with its strong rhythm and use of light and shade to achieve dramatic and grandiose effects. The markets formed a vast exedra with two storeys, flanked by two smaller ones, all occupied by shops.

Returning to Via dei Fori Imperiali, which leads to the Colosseum, we note the statues of the emperors, each placed in front of the Forum built by him.

The next Forum reached is the **Forum of Caesar**, marked by the bronze statue of Julius Caesar who ordered it to be built when the Roman Forum was no longer large enough. It was inaugurated in 46 B.C., but underwent various restorations and alterations in imperial times. The **Temple of Venus Genetrix** once stood there, which Caesar dedicated to her, since he claimed descent from her, and because she had often helped him in the wars.

Only three columns of the temple remain, raised on a high base.

The **Basilica Argentaria**, dating from the latter years of the Empire, stands nearby, and was used for the meetings of bankers and businessmen.

The **Forum of Augustus** was erected to commemorate the Battle of Philippi, in which Augustus defeated Brutus and Cassius, Caesar's murderers; this battle marked the beginning of his complete ascendancy and hence of the establishment of the empire. Very little of this Forum remains, although the structures of some of its buildings can still be identified and some columns are still standing.

Next to it is the **Forum of Nerva**, which has almost entirely disappeared, apart from a few columns, commonly known as the "colonnacce", surmounted by a fine frieze.

We then get a glimpse of the **Forum of Vespasian**, already mentioned during the visit to the Roman Forum.

We next visit the **Church of the Saints Cosma and Damian**, which, as already stated, was in part made out of the remains of the Templum Sacrae Urbis. In the apse are some mosaics dating from the end of the 6th

32

VIA FORI IMPERIALI

century; the rest of the church has rich baroque ornamentation.

Proceeding along the Via dei Fori Imperiali, the majestic mass of the **Basilica of Maxentius** comes into view. Its building was completed by Constantine in 312. Of this imposing pile, only one nave remains, with vaults as much as 25 metres high (those of the central nave reached a height of 53 metres), with a fine coffered ceiling. It is altogether a stupendous specimen of the monumental style achieved by Roman architecture, and of the solemnity with which they sought to endow every single building of imperial Rome, as a manifestation of the greatness and power of the city and its immense empire.

It should be noted that the Basilica had two entrances, one of them towards the Colosseum, the other onto the Via Sacra.

Today important musical events are held in the Basilica of Maxentius. From the Basilica of Maxentius the **Church of Santa Francesca Romana** can be reached, also known as Santa Maria Nova. It too can boast of ancient origins, as is the case with almost all the basilicas and churches of Rome. It was first built, in fact, in the 10th century, but nothing of its ancient structure now remains, owing to the continuous restorations, which have given a completely new appearance, predominantly in the style of the 17th century, especially as regards the façade. In the interior, pieces dating from the 12th and 13th century can be seen, such as for instance, the fine Cosmatic pavement. The Campanile too, is the original 12th century one. On the other hand, the **Tomb of Pope Gregory XI**, who put an end to the exile at Avignon, dates from Renaissance times.

The Church is part of a monastery, which now houses the **Antiquarium Forense**, or Museum of the Forum, where many remains concerning the history of Rome, especially the Fora, are displayed, as well as the things brought to light in the ancient necropolis already visited during our tour of the Roman Forum.

After visiting this church, we proceed to the remains of the **Temple of Venus and Rome**, built by the Emperor Hadrian in 135 A.D., in honour of the patron goddess of Rome and of the family of the Caesars. The temple, restored by Maxentius, consisted of two cells with adjoining apses and façades facing the Forum and colosseum respectively.

Today the ground plan of the temple has been restored and can be identified by means of the green plants that mark the site of its most important architectural features.

The Via dei Fori Imperiali, followed so far, leads to the Colosseum, which could already be glimpsed in the distance at the beginning of this itinerary.

THE COLOSSEUM

Is undoubtedly the best known of the monuments of ancient Rome. Its real name is the Flavian Amphitheatre; in fact, the name "Colosseum" was given to it later, for what precise reason is not known. It is generally assumed that this second appellation may perhaps be derived from a colossal statue of Nero which stood near it, to be exact, at the foot of the Palatine. Moreover, the architect of this amazing building, unmatched in Roman art, is unknown. It must, however, be admitted that, in the case of almost all the ancient works of art, we know litle more than what meets our eye today.

The Colosseum stands where the Palatine, Caelian and Oppian hills meet, on the spot where there was formerly a swampy lake, later drained.

A PLASTIC MODEL OF ROME BY I. GISMONDI - KEPT IN THE MUSEUM OF THE ROMAN CIVILIZATION ➤

The building dates from the imperial period, the exact date being 70 A.D., but it was not inaugurated until 80 A.D. However, its history does not end here, for it had to undergo many restorations and modifications, for its completion and embellishment.

The amphitheatre (that is to say, the doubling of the Greek theatre, which was semicircular in shape and was used for the performance of tragedies), is elliptical in shape, that is to say, virtually an elongated circle. It differs from the Greek theatre, of which it is the logical development, in having a double circumference, as the semicircle is repeated, and in addition, it is freestanding (while the Greek theatre rested on the hillside as its natural support). In fact, one encounters in this building, as in others of considerable importance, the absolute predominance of the curved line, which the Romans got from the Etruscans, but which they succeeded in exploiting, in order to achieve a new, grander and more solemn sense of space.

Although the Colosseum is today partly in ruins, its four orders of columns can still be clearly seen (in the four storeys): the first three consist of arcades separated by columns in the Doric, Ionic and Corinthian style respectively; the fourth is a solid wall pierced by windows. The top storey, higher than the others, more solid but less open, admirably crowns the whole building, as it were gathering together the spatial expansion of all its curves.

In the interior, the tiers could hold some 50.000 people.

A PLASTIC MODEL OF
ROME BY I GISMONDI
COLOSSEUM
A reconstruction
of its interior

THE COLOSSEUM
Imaginary reconstruction of the Colosseum, of the Meta Sudans of the Colossal bronze Statue of Nero

The greatest gladiatorial shows of antiquity were held in the amphiteatre. They were the favourite entertainment of the Romans, who had slaves specially trained to fight on another.

But that was not the only diversion popular in that civilisation: in addition to combats between men, they also organised fights between men and animals, and these were certainly among the most cruel. The latter were skillfully organised: the arena was made to look like a hill, a wood, or some other natural setting in order to afford the illusion of an actual hunt. In fact, shows of this kind were called "hunts".

But the technique and imagination of the Romans did not stop here. In fact, the Colosseum was also used for staging naval battles in miniature. For this purpose, the arena was filled with water by carefully devised me-

thods, and fierce battles were tought to the bitter end on this artificial lake.

The history of the Colosseum is, however, bound up with still more atracious events, for here the first Christians were martyred, and the time when the Christian religion was still prohibited by the laws of the state. Accordingly, all those sentenced to death for belonging to this religion were killed in this arena, providing the Roman public with a new sensation and new emotions.

Hence the Colosseum was an ideal place of entertainment, attracting enormous crowds from the whole of Rome as well as from neighbouring towns. It should, moreover, be remembered that the large amphitheatre possessed the most up-to-date installations for the rapid performance of the games. The underground passages and tunnels, by which men and beasts were intro-

THE COLOSSEUM   Inside - Reconstruction of a hunt of wild animals

duced into the arena, can still be seen, as well as the devices for transforming the arena into a lake, etc.

In addition, the Colosseum was provided with a special means of covering against bad weather, no longer to be seen; it was a particular device to spread a large awning above the building when need arose.

The present ruined state of the Colosseum is due not only to natural causes, but also to the plundering by noble families and art lovers, who carried off large amounts of valuable material to adorn their villas and palaces.

In conclusion, it may be said that this amazing amphitheatre is one of the most elaborate and majestic monuments of Roman art; it is above all the measure of the genius of the might of this civilisation.

Next, the **Arch of Constantine** is reached, where the Via Sacra came to an end. Built in 313 A.D., to celebrate Constantine's victories, it resembles the Arch of Septimius Severus, but is more monumental and more sculptural in conception, owing to the livelier movement of the surfaces, especially in the upper part. It is one of the last important achievements of Roman architecture, which from now on was to spread increasingly to the various provinces, while at Rome and in Italy the new Palaeo-Christian art develops. Near the Arch of Constantine there is a fountain in the shape of a cone, the **Meta Sudans**, where according to tradition the gladiators used to wash on leaving the Colosseum.

At the end of Via dei Fori Imperiali, some slabs of Travertine mark the place where stood the **Colossus of Nero**, an enormous statue which probably gave the Colosseum its name.

THE COLOSSEUM « Pollice Verso »

The gladiatoral combats were undoubtedly the most exciting. Perhaps they came down to the Romans from the Etruscans, who were their masters in many other things.

The gladiators (so called because they fought with the « gladius » or short sword), were mostly slaves and criminals, and there were also men who had voluntarily chosen this profession to earn money. They were trained in special schools (the one at Capua was particularly famous), under the guidance of a trainer. There were various types of combat: one of the most famous was the duel between the « retiarius » and the « secutor ». This was a fight between a gladiator armed with a net, in which he tried to entangle his opponent, and a trident with which to herass and kill him, and another gladiator armed with helmet, sword and shield, who tried to pursue and overcome his adversary. At the end of the fight the one who had been defeated asked the people for mercy, and they decided his fate: if they turned their thumbs down, it meant death.

CIRCUS MAXIMUS The Last Prayer

The Circus Maximus was built by Tarquinius Priscus, and later enlarged and reconstructed by Julius Caesar. It was used for all kinds of spectacles and held as many as 100.000 spectators.

The obelisks which now stand in Piazza del Popolo and in Piazza San Giovanni in Laterano came from there.

It was in the Circus Maximus, rather than in the Colosseum, that the Romans witnessed the torments of the Christians who were the victims of many persecutions. The names of many emperors are linked with these appalling events, which gave them an unenviable fame. Among the persecutions most notorious for the number of victims and for their cruelty, are those of Nero in 64 A.D., Domitian, Trajan, Septimius Severus, Decius, Valerian and Diocletian.

The last was known as the « great persecution ».

ARCH OF CONSTANTINE
Reconstruction

ARCH OF CONSTANTINE

THE PALATINE

Is one of the seven hills of Rome; it had three summits, two of which formed the so-called "Roma quadrata", the original nucleus of the city, contained, according to tradition, in the square of the furrow traced by Romulus. In addition to the **Temples of the Magna Mater and of Victory**, dating form the third century B.C., the villas of noble families were thereafter built on it, as well as great palaces in the period of the empire, such as the **Palace of Augustus** for instance, part of which survives in the **House of Livia**, and that of **Tiberius**.

The **Flavian Palace** and the **House of Augustus**, built during the Flavian dynasty, were architecturally conceived as a monumental and imposing whole. Other emperors enlarged and embellished the Palatine Hill with many buildings, such as the **Stadium** and the **Baths**, in addition to the majestic **Septizonium** erected by Septimius Severus, which proudly overlooks the Appian Way.

The Palatine however, was destined to undergo further enlargement and transformation over the centuries, so as to include even Christian buildings, as e.g. the **Church of San Cesario** and a monastery. It underwent a fundamental transformation in the 16th century at the hands of the Farnese family, which made it its residence after buying some of the land on which it built a magnificent villa, while the surrounding area became a splendid garden. The Farnese family interested themselves in bringing to light a large part of the archaeological remains.

We owe the present appearance of the Palatine to the work of outstanding archaelogists, such as **Rosa** and **Boni**.

The Palatine is reached by way of the Clivus Palatinus, which starts near the Arch of Titus.

Then a staircase leads to the **Farnese Gardens**, created in the 16th century by the Farnese family, as already mentioned. They are still to this day a place of enchantment. In their midst stands the **Casino Farnese**, the fine villa where the family lived.

MARCELLO THEATRE

Around these gardens there are many archeological remains of the buildings which from Rome's earliest days, dominated the Palatine: the **House of Tiberius** (of which there remains a row of massive arcades); the **Temple of the Magna Mater** (one of the oldest, now almost wholly destroyed), and the **Statue of Cybele**; the **Stairs of Cacus** (one of the ways up to the Palatine); the **town walls** (perhaps the earliest in Rome); the **House of Livia** (well preserved; Augustus had it built in order to live there); the **Cryptoporticus** of Nero (an underground passage which was connected to the Golden House); the **Flavian Palace** (built, as has been said, for the emperors of the Flavian house. It is so well preserved that even to this day one can make out the whole plan of this magnificent palace): the **House of Augustus** (dating from the same time), partly occupied by a monastery now used as a **Museum**; the **Stadium of Domitian** (for his private use); the **Baths of Septimius Severus** (with their imposing architecture); the Paedagogium (a school for future politicians).

From Piazza Venezia one takes Via del Teatro Marcello, above which rises on the left the Capitoline Hill and the tufa mass of the Tarpeian Rock.

To the right, in Piazza Campitelli, stands the **Church of Santa Maria in Campitelli** with its 17th century façade by Rainaldi. On the altar inside there is a beautiful 13th

THE FOUNTAIN OF THE TURTLES

century enamel of the Virgin.

At the far end of the square, in Via dei Funari, is the **Church of Santa Caterina dei Funari**, of ancient foundation, but almost entirely rebuilt in the 16th century. It is called after the Roman ropemakers, who had their workshops in this area.

Next comes Piazza Mattei with **Palazzo Mattei**, built early in the 17th century by Maderno for Cardinal Asdrubale Mattei. There are interesting frescoes by Domenichino in the interior. In the square is the charming **Tortoise Fountain** by Landini and Della Porta (1585), most graceful in its conception and execution, especially in the slim figures of the youths holding up the tortoises who are climbing up to drink in the upper basin.

Taking Via di Sant'Angelo in Pescheria from Piazza Santa Maria in Campitelli, one can reach the **Portico di Ottavia**, erected by Augustus in honour of his sister Octavia, and altered by Septimius Severus. Its entrance can still be seen, with the portico which serves as the atrium of the **Church of Sant'Angelo in Pescheria** (a fine fresco by Gozzoli in the interior). West of the Portico of Octavia lies the Jewish quarter, known as the **Ghetto** with its many little shops full of all kinds of goods, giving the impression of a bazaar.

Returning to Via del Teatro Marcello, one comes to the **Theatre of Marcellus**, from which the street takes

THE SYNAGOGUE

its name. When completed, the theatre was dedicated to Marcellus, a nephew of Augustus, who met an early death. The building as we see it today has been partly altered by the superstructures added in later centuries, but the general outline of its original architecture is still clearly visible, with its powerful series of three rows of arcades (of which only two remain today), and the deep barrel vaults giving a marked effect of light and shade. This theatre has an important place in the history of Roman art, since it inaugurates a completely new kind of theatre, quite different in conception from the Greek theatre, which, since it was built into the hillside as has already been mentioned, could not demonstrate well the power of the curved line rising freely into space. The 16th century **Palazzo Orsini** occupies the third storey of the Theatre of Marcellus.

The columns in front of the theatre are the remaining ones of the **Temple of Apollo Sosianus**, of very ancient origin, but also altered several times.

The nearby **Church of San Nicola in Carcere** rests on the remains of three temples: it has been rebuilt several times. The columns and bases of these temples can be seen built into its walls. In the interior is a beautiful **Madonna** by **Antoniazzo Romano**.

Turning off Via del Taetro Marcello, one can arrive at the bank of the Tiber, near the **Tiber Island**. This is a small island formed by the alluvial deposits of the river; it has the characteristic shape of a ship. In ancient times, **a Temple of Aesculapius**, the god of medicine, was built here in gratitude for delivery from a terrible plague; today a hospital stands there. The ancient **Church of St. Bartholomew the Apostle** is very interesting; its fine campanile and the well-head in the interior are original.

After returning to Via del Teatro Marcello and passing the **House of Crescenzio**, a kind of medieval fortress, one comes to the **Forum Boarium** with a wealth of archaeological remains. Here stands the **Temple of For-**

TIBERINA ISLE

THE CHURCH OF S. MARIA IN COSMEDIN ➤

tuna Virilis, also called the Temple of the **Mater Matuta**, still showing Greek influence, and the **Temple of Vesta** (so called because of its similarity to the real Temple of Vesta, from which it has taKen over the circular ground plan. It has a Corinthian colonnade, and its architecture is still strongly influenced by Greek art, although typical elements of the beginnings of Roman art are already to be discerned): the **Arch of Janus Quadrifons**, built in the time of Constantine at a crossroads, to afford shelter to the people visiting the market.

The **Church of San Giorgio in Velabro** is next visited; it is of ancient origin and still preserves the portico and campanile of the 12th century. In the interior is a 13th century fresco by **P. Cavallini**, representing the **"Virgin and Saints"**. Near the Church is the **Arco degli Argentari** dating from the third century A.D., and opposite, the **Cloaca Maxima**. This is a channel built in the time of the kings and reconstructed in the Republican period, to carry off the water of the Tiber from the surrounding hills so that it should not become stagnant and make the ground marshy. It is undoubtedly one of the most imposing achievements of the advanced engineering of the Romans.

The **Church of Santa Maria in Cosmedin** dates from the 6th century, but underwent frequent alterations. Today it is an example of a medieval church with the basilica ground plan. It has an interesting door with a 9th century forecourt. The large mask on the left of the portico has been called the **"Bocca della Verità"** (the "Mouth of Truth") because, according to popular superstition, it bites the hand of anyone who tells lies.

THE TEMPLE OF VESTA   THE MOUTH OF TRUTH ➤

Our itinerary now leaves the centre of Rome, to go in search of notable art treasures. By way of Via di Santa Sabina one reaches the **Church of Santa Sabina**. It is one of the early examples of Palaeo-Christian art, and one of the few churches whose original structure still remains almost intact. The building dates from the 5th century A.D. and possesses all the characteristic features of churches with the basilica plan. Its three naves are divided by a series of most elegant columns with Corinthian capitals surmounted by round arches. The swift rhythm of the rows of columns leads the glance to the apse, where the movement comes to a standstill in the curve of its walls. The trussed wooden ceiling follows the design of Early Christian art. Originally the church was covered with mosaics, none of which now remain; the one in the apse is a late imitation.

Passing the **Church of Sant'Alessio** and the **Villa of the Knights of Malta**, one proceeds by Via di San Saba, noting the fine Romanesque façade of the **Church of San Saba** with its beautiful Cosmatesque doorway. In the interior are other interesting works of art. By way of Piazza Albania and Via della Piramide, after the **Porta Ostiense** in the Aurelian Walls, one comes to the famous **Pyramid of Caius Cestius** which contains the tomb of a Roman magistrate.

Nearby is the **Protestant Cemetery** (with the graves of several famous foreign writers), and, along Via Ostiense, the remains of a necropolis dating from the Republican period and later years.

The **Basilica of St. Paul without the Walls** is reached next.

Unfortunately this church, which was one of the most important and largest of Christian churches, and above all, one of the first to be built (it goes back to the 4th century), can no longer be seen in its original condition, for it was completely destroyed by fire in the 19th century. It was rebuilt a few ears later, but, like everything remade, even if a perfect imitation of the original, it lacks warmth and has therefore lost its intrinsic beauty.

Actually, something of the ancient Basilica has remained, mostly decorations, like the mosaics of the triumphal arch (5th century), the **Altar Canopy** of **Arnolfo di Cambio** (12th century), etc. Moreover, the picturesque 13th century cloister has remained intact. (photo on the side). However, there can be no doubt that the spirit which animated the architecture of this Basilica, which was one of the earliest of Christendom, has been almost completely lost; what remains today is the general outline which gives an impression of grandeur and solemnity.

EUR

Proceeding along Via Ostiense and then taking Via Laurentina, after about two kilometres, the **Abbey of the Three Fountains** is reached; it was built on the spot where, according to tradition, St. Paul was beheaded.

To the right of the Abbey stretches a vast, recently built-up area: it is E.U.R., a modern residential quarter, originally intended to house the Roman World Exhibition which was to have been opened on April 21, 1942. Owing to the outbreak of the Second World War, this Exhibition was not held, and the district was used for other buildings, such as houses, huge palaces for exhibitions, congresses, cultural manifestations, as well as sports halls (the famous Sports Palace should be noted).

In short, E.U.R. might be called the "Forum" of present-day Rome.

Among its best known buildings we mention: the **Sports Palace** by Pier Luigi Nervi, the **Palazzo della Civiltà del Lavoro** (Palace of Labour), the **Congress Hall** and the large **Church of St. Peter and St. John**.

The **Palace of Roman Civilisation** contains the Museum of the same name, with a vast documentation giving a picture of life as it was lived in Rome over the centuries: above all one gets an idea of the customs and habits with particular reference to the imperial period. There are also models and facsimiles reproducing the aspect of the city at the time of the emperors, in addition to more specialised historical documentation or that concerning the development of Christianity.

In Piazzale Italia, there is moreover the **Museo delle Arti e Tradizioni Popolari**, containing interesting collections of folklore material illustrating various aspects of the habits, costumes and traditions of Italy; the collection gives the visitor an idea of the colour, spontaneity and vitality, at times somewhat exuberant, of the Italian people.

The **Pigorini Prehistoric Ethnographical Museum** has a rich collection of ancient material from Italy and elsewhere, belonging to prehistoric civilisations and later periods up to the Middle Ages.

PANORAMA

A VIEW BY NIGHT

THE SPORT PALACE

THE PALACE OF THE
CIVILTA' ITALIANA

THE CONGRESS PALACE

This itinerary also starts from Piazza Venezia, and after reaching the Colosseum near the Arch of Constantine, follows Via San Gregorio, formerly known as Via dei Trionfi, which corresponds to the ancient Via Triumphalis, along which passed the splendid triumphal processions held in honour of commanders returning victorious from some important enterprise of war. To the right are the slopes of the Palatine, and on the left can be seen the apse of the Church of St. John and St. Paul, to which a visit will shortly be made.

Passing beyond Piazza del Circo Massimo, one comes to the ancient **Church of St. Gregory**, dating from the 6th century, but rebuilt in the 8th, and again altered in later periods.

In the interior, likewise restored, there are two fine paintings by **Guido Reni** and **Domenichino** respectively.

The Clivo di Scauro climbs up to the left of the Church, a picturesque street which also leads to the Church of St. John and St. Paul (to be described later).

Going down again to Piazza del Circo Massimo, a 16th century villa, the **Vignola**, can be seen on the left, and in the centre the **Obelisc of Axum**.

The **Paseggiata Archeologica** extends towards the Aventine, opening up to us another beautiful and interesting part of Rome. It was planned by Baccelli.

One first reaches the **Porta Capena**, and then the **Church of Santa Balbina** (of ancient origin, but partly restored: in it are preserved fine works of art of the 13th and 15th centuries).

Thus one comes to the famous **Baths of Caracalla**, one of the most imposing monuments remaining today; even in Roman times these Baths were famous for their size and splendour. They were built at the beginning of the third century by the Emperor Caracalla, after whom they are called. They had room for a vast number of people and had many well equipped rooms and halls. Above all, there were rooms for actual baths, divided into cold, warm and hot baths. In addition to these, moreover, there was a series of places for other purposes for the relaxation of the Romans who visited the baths: gardens, libraries and gymnasia. Undoubtedly the Baths were very important for the Romans, but when they had fallen into disuse, in a certain sense, they found their continuation in the architecture of the

CARACALLA BATHS

ANCIENT APPIAN WAY

early Christian churches which took their ground plan, not only from the Roman basilica, but also from the baths. This of course applies to all those sacred buildings, such as churches and baptisteries with a circular plan.

Leaving the Baths of Caracalla and proceeding towards Porta di San Sebastiano, one steps to take a look at the **Tomb of the Scipios**, excavated in the tufa like the Etruscan hypogea. The façade of the tomb made it look like a temple, and it was in fact revered like a temple by the Romans who always kept fresh the memory of this famous family.

Porta San Sebastiano stands at the end of the street of the same name, and beyond the walls starts the famous Appian Way; in fact, the Gate was originally called the Porta Appia. With its two fine medieval towers, it is undoubtedly the most majestic of the gates in the Aurelian Walls.

Before going along the Appian Way, by skirting the Aurelian Walls, one can reach **Porta Latina** and, going back towards the city centre, the **Oratory of San Giovanni in Oleo** of the 16th century, and finally, climb the **Caelian Hill**.

From the Caelian Hill, via Piazza della Navicella, and then by way of Via di Santo Stefano Rotondo, one comes to the circular **Church of Santo Stefano Rotondo**, built about the 5th century A.D.

Next comes the **Church of St. John and St. Paul**, built over the remains of some ancient Roman houses in very early times, but completely rebuilt in the Middle Ages (the fine Campanile of this period still stands), and again in later centuries.

Returning to Porta San Sebastiano, from which the above detour started, one takes the ancient APPIAN WAY.

This is an exceedingly and rewarding walk, and is one of the favourite romantic excursions of the Romans.

The Appian Way was the most important of the ancient Roman roads, and was built in 312 B.C. by the Consul Appius Claudius. It linked Rome with Southern Italy, going as far as Tarentum.

Moreover, it bears testimony to the steady and rapid expansion of the political and commercial power of Rome which, right from the beginning of its history, exercised a quite exceptional rule. This dominion was preserved and improved by means of a number of peaceful enterprises, such as the building of roads, the aim of which was not only to facilitate communications, but above all to speed up and increase trade and cultural exchanges with other civilisations.

Along the Appian Way, with its lovely natural surroundings, funeral monuments were erected, and a number of catacombs were dug early in the Christian area. The ancient paving is preserved in many stretches.

At the beginning of the walk, one comes first of all to the **Church of Domine Quo Vadis** (Lord, whither goest Thou?), so called after the words spoken, according to tradition, by St. Peter to Our Lord.

The side road, Via Ardeatina, leads to the **Fosse Ardeatine**, where 320 Italians are buried, who were killed as a reprisal by the Germans during the last war. This great burial ground, containing the bodies of so many men, women and children, still bears eloquent testimony to the horrors of the war. Solemn ceremonies are held here every year to commemorate the sacrifice of so many who gave their lives, like thousands of others.

About one and a half Kilometres along the Appian Way are the **Catacombs of St. Calixtus.** Like many others in Rome and its surroundings, these Catacombs were a place of refuge of the early Christians. The rise of Christianity was not uncontested; on the contrary, it was opposed because it was considered a force hostile to the state, damaging to the institutions and to the very security of the empire. This is understandable when one considers that a religious movement of this kind, which preached the equality of all and respect for the human personality, must certainly have been inconvenient to the rulers and men in the government. It must not be forgotten that in Roman society, as in all the preceding civilisations, slavery was practised, and that in any case, neither servants nor foreigners enjoyed the same rights as Roman citizens.

For this reason, all followers of the new religion, in its early years and for some centuries after, had to hide, practising their rites in secret and meeting in secret. This was the origin of the catacombs, a series

CATACOMBS OF ST. CALIXTUS
Crypt of St. Cecilia (2nd. - 3nd. century)

CATACOMBS OF DOMITILLA

TOMB OF CECILIA METELLA

of corridors, warrens, rooms and underground sep-
ulchres, which for centuries were the refuge of the
Christians as well as their early, marvellous church.
Indeed, with the years, underneath the pagan Rome,
monumental, solemn and majestic, a second Rome gradually coming into existence a Christian Rome, poor
and humble, enveloped in darkness and mysticism.
These two cities, one above the other, swarmed with
life, but in each of them, there was a completely
different life and civilisation.

The Catacombs of St. Calixtus are undoubtedly the
most important at Rome; they are called after the
Deacon Calixtus, who enlarged the labyrinth of galleries
and crypts already in existence, making them the abode
and cemetery of the Christians and Popes of the time.

Without listing in detail the remains to be found
here, it need only be said that most of the tombs are
those of 3rd century popes, and that there are crypts
of great artistic value owing to the ancient frescoes
which are still in excellent condition.

Taking the turn of Via Appia Pignatelli, one comes
to the **Catacombs of S. Pretextatus**. On the Appian Way
are also the **Jewish Catacombs** and those of **S. Domitilla**.

Further on one comes to the **Church of St. Sebastian**
with the adjoining Catacombs.

Beyond the **Circus of Maxentius**, dating from the
4th century A.D., one finds the famous **Tomb of Cecilia
Metella**, a sepulchral monument of the second half of
the first century A.D., inspired by the early Italian
house. For several more Kilometres, the road continues
between tombs and graves, bearing testimony to the
lives of many ancient Romans.

The road now comes to the remains of the **Villa
of the Quintili**, dating from the time of Augustus. The
estate, with its palaces, nymphaea, arcades and store-
houses, belonged to the wealthy family of the Quintili,
who were killed and had their property confiscated
at the order of the Roman Emperor Commodus.

At the 8th Kilometre one comes to **Casal Rotondo**, a
large mausoleum in which Valerius Cotta was buried
at the time of Augustus. On the level surface of the
tomb, a farmhouse with a small garden was later built.
Other ruins are scattered nearby in the Roman Cam-
pagna, such as remains of aqueducts, Patrician villas,
medieval fortifications and sepulchral monuments.

CHURCH OF SAN PIETRO IN VINCOLI

From Piazza Venezia, by way of Via dei Fori Imperiali, Via Cavour and Via San Francesco di Paola, one arrives through a subway at the **Church of San Pietro in Vincoli**, so called because the chains (vincula) of the Saint, with which he was bound as a prisoner, are kept there. The Church, dating from very early times, has been restored and altered several times, one of the architects being Fontana.

In the interior, divided into three naves by columns taken from earlier buildings, is preserved one of the best known of Italian works of art; the **Tomb of Julius II** by Michelangelo. The monument realises only in part the original plan of the artist, who had conceived it on a much larger scale and with many more statues. In fact, after the death of Pope Julius II, the patrons reconsidered the project, with the result that it was considerably reduced. This Tomb was to have been a solemn, majestic monument, uniting architecture and sculpture. Only a few statues of this concept remain today, such as the very famous Moses, which conveys some idea of the sculptural force and energy that would have inspired the whole. The Church contains other interesting works by **Bregno, Domenichino** and **Guercino**.

CHURCH OF ST. PETER IN VINCULIS

The Moses of Michelangelo ➤

CHAIRS OF ST. PETER

CHURCH OF ST. PETER IN VINCULIS   Interior

BASILICA OF SANTA MARIA MAGGIORE

Returning to Via Cavour and then taking Via Lanza, one climbs the **Esquiline** another of the seven hills of Rome, where stands the **Church of San Martino ai Monti**, built by Pietro da Cortona.

Leaving by Via delle Sette Sale, one may go on to the Park of Trajan on the slopes of the **Oppian Hill** to the right.

This hill, which can also be easily reached from the Colosseum, contains the remains of the **Golden House**, the sumptuous residence intended by Nero to become the new Imperial Palace after the fire of Rome. It remained unfinished and was partly destroyed or covered over by Trajan for the building of his new Baths. It has now been excavated to reveal a vast labyrinth of rooms with remarkable fresco paintings of mythological scenes, attributed to a certain Fabullus and highly esteemed in later times.

After returning to the Esquiline and crossing Via Lanza, after Via San Martino ai Monti, one takes Via di Santa Prassede on the left in order to reach the **Church of Santa Prassede**, built in the 5th century, but rebuilt several times, although some of its original structure and decoration still remain. Moreover, the Church has a wealth of mosaics and relics, amongst which, in a niche, there is a pillar brought from Jerusalem by the Crusaders, to which, according to tradition, Christ was bound to be scourged. There is also a stone on which the Saint used to lie, and in the Crypt a sarcophagus containing the bones of Santa Prassede and her sister, Santa Pudenziana.

BASILICA OF ST. MARIA MAGGIORE

BASILICA OF ST. MARIA MAGGIORE - Interior

MOSAIC OF THE APSIS ➤

Continuing along Via di Santa Prassede, one arrives at Piazza Santa Maria Maggiore, in the centre of which is a Column brought here at the time of Pope Paul V from the Basilica of Constantine. In the 17th century, a bronze statue of the Virgin and Child by Berthelot was placed at its top.

We are now facing the great **Basilica of Santa Maria Maggiore**, built by Pope Liberius in order to commemorate the place where, following a vision of the Virgin, he found snow in the month of August. This was in the 5th century, and the Church was built as a great early Christian Basilica, one of the largest of the time. In spite of the many restorations and transformations it has undergone in the course of the centuries, the ground plan with its three naves, divided by rows of trabeated columns, remains unchanged so that even today one still gets the general impression of the original conception. Among the major and most important transformations from the artistic point of view must be mentioned the two fine façades, one facing Piazza di Santa Maria Maggiore, the other at the opposite end. The real façade is that designed by Fuga in 1743, which seems to be embedded in the side wings, but nevertheless stands out from them, thanks to its slight projection and certain pictorial and stylistic touches isolating it from the rest of the masonry. The other façade, generally known as the Tribuna of Santa Maria Maggiore, rises above a long flight of steps, and is the work of Rainaldi (17th century). It too is very interesting for the exceptional balance of its animated parts and an harmonious merging of the horizontal and vertical lines.

The interior of the Church is truly majestic, and, as has been said, preserves to a large extent the atmosphere of the early Christian basilicas.

It contains remarkable works of art, dating from the time when the basilica was built, as well as many masterpieces from later times. The fine, 16th century coffered ceiling (perhaps the work of Giuliano da Maiano), which has replaced the earlier one deserves special notice; also the Cosmatesque pavement, the 5th century mosaics decorating the triumphal arch and the architraves (the latter with scenes from the Old Testament).

BASILICA OF SAN GIOVANNI IN LATERANO

From Piazza Venezia, taking Via dei Fori Imperiali, after passing the Colosseum, one turns into Via di San Giovanni in Laterano, on the left of which stands the **Basilica of San Clemente**, one of the oldest and most interesting in Rome. The Basilica consists of two churches, one on top of the other, the lower dating from the 4th century A.D. The other was built on top of this in the 12th century, mainly out of materials from the earlier one. Both churches are beautiful and interesting: the upper one, visited first, still retains intact the aspect of a basilica as well as its original decorations, apart from the ceiling, which is of recent date. However, the lower church is more intimate and appealing, not only for its architecture, which has remained almost untouched, but also for the beautiful mosaic decoration.

Another interesting church is that of the **Quattro Santi Coronati** (reached by turning into Via dei Cerqueti, and then Via dei Santi Coronati), which has a fine Romanesque campanile and a handsome cloister. The Cosmatesque pavement and the crypt are worth noting.

Then one comes to Piazza San Giovanni in Laterano, dominated by the **Egyptian Obelisk**. On the right is the **Baptistery of St. John**, one of the first be built and one of the earliest Christian buildings with a circular ground plan. It dates from the 4th century. In the centre is the basalt baptismal font, and round it, beyond the columns, the chapels, some of which are specially interesting because they are covered with 4th and 5th century mosaics.

One now visits the great **Basilica of San Giovanni in Laterano**, the first great Christian church, since it was built next to the Lateran Palace which was the first gift of the Emperor Constantine. The church was of course altered and enlarged several times by famous architects, among whom are Borromini and Fontana.

The side façade of the Church, surmounted by two bell towers, was designed in the 16th century by Fontana. The main façade, however, is the work of Galilei, solemn and majestic in conception with its powerful single order of columns, crowned by a prominent archi-

BASILICA OF ST. JOHN IN LATERAN

BASILICA OF ST. JOHN
IN LATERAN   The Cloister

BASILICA OF ST. JOHN
IN LATERAN - Interior

trave, surmounted in turn by 12 statues.

The five doors, the last of which is the Holy Door, give access to the Atrium. The very impressive interior is 130 metres long and has five aisles: it contains many art treasures and important historical monuments.

Only the most important works of art are mentioned here, above all the fine Cosmatesque pavement and the richly decorated 16th century ceiling. In the niches of the pillars of the central aisle are the statues of the Apostles by pupils of Bernini, and stuccoes by Algardi (18th century).

A fresco by Giotto should also be noted, depicting "Boniface VII proclaiming the Holy Year" (1st pillar), the fine 14th century canopy on the Papal Altar, the 13th century mosaics in the apse, and the transept by Della Porta. A visit should also be paid to the attractive and picturesque cloisters, built by Vassalletto (1230), with little arches resting on twin columns encrusted with mosaics. In the cloisters are numerous fragments from the first church.

Beside the Church stands the great **Lateran Palace**: it was the residence of the Popes at the time of Constantine, that is to say at the time when he donated it, and so it remained until the 14th century, when the Popes transferred their residence to Avignon for some seventy years. After they had moved their residence to the Vatican Palace, the Lateran became the seat of the Lateran Museums. In the meantime the old building had been altered and almost completely rebuilt by Fontana (16th century).

The Museums are divided into three sections: the **Museo Profano** (containing various works of the pre-Christian period), the **Museo Cristiano** (with a wealth of historical documentation of Christianity), the **Museo Missionario Etnologico** (with interesting exhibits showing the missionary activity of many priests, and above all, documentation concerning the history of peoples, civilisations, customs and traditions).

Across the square is the **Scala Santa**, which, according to tradition, Christ ascended on his way to meet Pilate. At the top of it is the **Chapel of San Lorenzo**, or the **Sancta Sanctorum**, containing a picture of Christ said not to be painted by human hand. It should further be noted that the Chapel is all that remains of the original Lateran Palace.

Returning to Piazza San Giovanni, one sees opposite the Basilica of San Giovanni, the monument of **St. Francis of Assisi.** At one end of the Piazza di Porta San Giovanni are the Aurelian Walls, pierced by the ancient **Porta San Giovanni.** Beyond it starts the Via Appia Nuova, leading from Rome to the attractive Castelli Romani (Alban Hills), one of the most rewarding excursions in the surroundings. From here one may reach not only the Ciampino Airport, but also Albano, Castel Gandolfo (the Pope's summer residence), Marino, Genzano, Aricia, Frascati and the picturesque Lake of Albano (sometimes called the Lake of Castel Gandolfo, with a touch of local patriotism on both sides). Roaming among these "Castelli", one encounters once more something of Rome's local colour, that is to say of the less solemn and stately Rome — the atmosphere of jovial Rome, fond of good wine (the wine of the Castelli is world-famous), and a good plate of spaghetti, and after such a good meal, a sing-song together to the accompaniment of an old guitar. These songs too are typically Roman, the ditties drowned in another glass of good wine to clear the throat.

The excursion to the Castelli is most interesting, especially for those who would like to rediscover the real local colour of the city and all its traditions. Our itinerary, however, must be confined to Rome, and so, continuing from Piazza di San Giovanni in Laterano, one goes to the nearby Piazza di Santa Croce in Gerusalemme, where the **Church of Santa Croce in Gerusalemme** stands, dating from the 4th century, but completely rebuilt in the 17th and 18th century, as can be seen from the baroque façade, with the strongly marked rhythm of its parts, and from the interior. The campanile, on the other hand, is Romanesque. The Church takes its name from the relic of the Cross preserved in it.

By Via Eleniana one reaches Piazza Maggiore with the **Porta Maggiore**, dating from 52 A.D.

Further on, along the Via Prenestina, is the **Basilica di Porta Maggiore**, only recently discovered, since it is below ground. Its decorations are very interesting.

THE HOLY STAIRCASE

At Porta Maggiore also starts Via Casilina, which after some three Kilometres, brings one to the **Catacombs of SS. Marcellinus and Petrus**.

Taking Via Cesare Battisti from Piazza Venezia, one skirts the 16th century Palazzo della Provincia, and enters Via Quattro Novembre, on the left of which, at the corner with Piazza dei SS. Apostoli, stands **Palazzo Colonna**. It was built by the Colonna Pope Martin V, and its present aspect dates from the 18th century. It is joined by four arches to Villa Colonna which is situated on the slopes of the Quirinal and has fine gardens around the ruins of the Temple of Serapis.

It contains the **Colonna Gallery**, with its wealth of masterpieces of art, among which we mention works by Veronese, L. Lotto, Tintoretto, Van Dyck, N. Alunno, Ribera, Rubens, Guercino, A. Carracci, Melozzo da Forlì and others, as well as outstanding frescoes and decorations.

The adjoining Church of the SS. Apostoli will be visited in one of the later itineraries.

Continuing along Via Quattro Novembre, having passed by the Market of Trajan, one reaches Piazza Magnapoli, where there are some remains of the Servian Wall, and, above the market, a 13th century tower, the **Torre delle Milizie**. The Emperor Henry VII lived here when he came to Rome.

Nearby is the 17th century **Church of Santa Caterina**, with its baroque façade.

Here begins the Via Nazionale, one of the most important and busiest streets of Rome. On the right one passes the building of the Banca d'Italia, and then on the left, the **Palazzo delle Esposizioni**, a 19th century building used today for important art exhibitions, among them the **"Quadriennale Nazionale d'Arte"**, the best known of all.

Next comes the **Church of San Vitale**, below street level. It is of very early origin, but little of the original structure can be seen owing to the many alterations and subsequent transformations.

In the **American Church of St. Paul**, not far from it, neo-Romanesque in style, there are interesting mosaics and a carillon-organ. A little further on, taking Via Firenze, one comes to the Opera House, where every year outstanding performances are given.

ESEDRA SQUARE

One now continues along Via Nazionale until one reaches Piazza Esedra (Piazza della Repubblica) with the **Fountain of the Naiads** in the centre, an elegant and harmonious work, designed by Rutelli at the beginning of this century.

The majestic ruins of the **Baths of Diocletian** serve as a background to Piazza Esedra; they were built in the 4th century A.D. and could accomodate some 3000 people. Thus they were much larger and commodious than the Baths of Caracalla, and display a really outstanding building technique, above all with regard to the functionality of the architecture and of all the installations.

In the 16th century Michelangelo was commissioned to adapt the ruins of the Baths to new purposes: thus the **Church of Santa Maria degli Angeli** was created, with the adjoining monastery and the later the **National Museum of Rome** (Museo delle Terme).

Michelangelo's project for the Church of Santa Maria degli Angeli was not entirely respected; in fact, it was considerably modified by Vanvitelli, who made significant alterations to the proportions and harmony of the whole building. However, the church has remained unfinished, and it is therefore difficult to give a definitive judgment on its final appearance. The Church contains many funeral monuments, including that of Salvator Rosa, painter, poet and musician, who led a brillant and adventurous life, and, in one of the transept chapels, the Tomb of Marshall Diaz and that of Carlo Marotta, designed by himself.

There are some very interesting 17th and 18th century paintings, among them a masterpiere by Subleyras (1748), "The Mass of S. Basil", and the "Fall of Simon Magus", by Pompeo Battoni (1760), as well as other important works, such as the "Martyrdom of St. Sebastian" by Domenichino.

In the rooms of the monastery belonging to the Carthusian Order, the **National Museum of Rome**, or Museo delle Terme, has been housed. It was started in the 19th century and is supplemented by the two small Museums placed in the two cloisters of the Monastery: the Cloister of the Certosa and the Great Cloister. Altogether, these museums contain a considerable number of works of art, all of them most interesting and important, not only for the history of art, but also for the history of a whole civilisation. There is a very rich collection of sculpture, sarcophagi and fragments of mosaics. Only a few of the best known works are mentioned here: the "Niobe" from the Gardens of Sallust, so called because the statue was found there (it dates from the 5th century and is probably an original): the "Venus of Cyrene", (a copy of a Greek statue of the 4th century B.C.); the "Discobolos", another very fine copy of the famous original; the "Girl of Anzio", a Hellenistic original of the 4th century; the "Ephebe", found at Subiaco, the "Pugilist resting" by Apollonius; the 5th century statue of Athens; the "Bathing Venus"; the "Ludovisi Throne"; the "Marble Altar from Ostia" of the 2nd century A.D. In addition, there are many wall paintings, fragments of mosaics and various busts and portraits.

Starting once more from Piazza Venezia and going to Largo Magnapoli, one turns from there into Via XXIX Maggio, which leads to the Quirinal. On the way, one comes to the 16th century **Church of San Silvestro al Quirinale** (with important works of art in the interior), **Villa Colonna** (already mentioned), and the **Palazzo Pallavicini Rospigliosi**, designed by Vasanzio. The interior is worth a special visit, as it contains the **Pallavicini Gallery** with very important works by Rubens, Salvator Rosa, Signorelli, Lorenzo Lotto, Poussin, Ribera, Van Dyck, and other great masters. Special mention should also be given to the fresco painting by Guido Reni, depicting **Aurora**, on the ceiling of the Casino of the Palace. It was commissioned from him by Cardinal Scipio Borghese, who had also entrusted him with the task of decorating the apse of a chapel in the Church of St. Gregory on the Caelian Hill. In these two works Guido Reni achieves wonderful balance and harmony.

On reaching the Piazza del Quirinale, one notes the **Fountain of the Dioscuri**. The imposing statues were found in the gardens of Constantine and brought here in the time of Sixtus V. They are two good Roman copies of Greek originals of the 4th to 5th century B.C. The Obelisk, taken from the Mausoleum of Augustus, was later erected between the two statues, and around it was placed the basin which previously stood in the Forum.

Since 1947 the **Quirinal Palace** has been the residence of the President of the Republic. It takes its name from the hill on which it is situated, the Quirinal which in turn is derived from Quirinus, the Sabine god of war. The building of the Palace was started in the 16th century by Pope Gregory XIII, on the place where formerly stood the villa of Cardinal Ippolito d'Este, and was completed only in the 18th century with the cooperation of many architects, including Bernini himself. Maderno and Fontana. The exterior of the building is in the Renaissance style, with a fine doorway by Maderno, who was also responsible for the Cappella Paolina inside, decorated with stuccoes. The elegant arcade around the courtyard is by Fontana, and the various rooms in the palace have a wealth of superb decorations, tapestries and paintings. The frescoes by Melozzo da Forlì and Guido Reni merit special mention.

To the right of the square stands the **Palazzo della Consulta**, designed by Fuga in the 18th century.

Continuing along Via del Quirinale, one comes to the **Church of Sant'Andrea al Quirinale** on the right, designed by Bernini about 1658. It is undoubtedly one of the most important examples of the master's art, and one of the most dynamic as far as concerns architecture. Although quite small, the Church has great spatial energy, deriving from its circular, or rather, elliptical shape. The dynamic tension of the lines here creates a whole which seems to extend beyond its limits, giving free rein to all its structural elements.

Further on, on the right, one reaches the **Church of San Carlino**, a building of great importance for the development of another artist, Borromini, Bernini's great rival. It too is small, but important as showing his conception of architecture. This Church gives us some idea of the different spirit that inspired the art of these two great masters of the 16th century. Above all, the interior of the church should be noted, where the elliptical ground plan, the dynamic tension of which has already been observed in Bernini, becomes more restless and still more sculptural in the search for delicate, luminous achievements.

Next one comes to the crossroads of the Four Fountains, a fine and characteristic conception. Four wide thoroughfares start from this point, ending in the Quirinal, the Esquiline and the Pincian Hills, and Porta Pia respectivelty. At the corners of the crossroads are the **Four Fountains**.

One now takes Via delle Quattro Fontane to reach Piazza Barberini, noting on the right the Palazzo Barberini, begun by Maderno, and later finished by Bernini, who added a central section protruding from the rest. Accordingly the façade is more marked, especially by the different articulation of the architectural mass of means of three large orders of arcades in the classicistic style. The palace houses the **National Gallery of Ancient Art**, containing many works of art (still in course of being rearranged), by Raphael, Fra Angelico, Tintoretto, Piero della Francesca, Simone Martini, and many others.

In Piazza Barberini stands Bernini's beautiful **Fountain with the Triton**.

From this square starts the famous, fashionable **Via Veneto**, at the beginning of which stands the **Fountain of the Bees**, likewise designed by Bernini for Pope Urban VIII, who wished to endow the area with one ornamental fountain and another for public use; in the latter the artist incorporated the motif of the bees, the heraldic emblem of Barberini family.

Via Veneto, which starts here, is certainly Rome's most famous street, frequented by the best known personalities of the world of entertainment and by the upper class of the city. On either side of it are luxury hotels and bars, which become very animated especially at night.

Via Veneto leads to Porta Pinciana. On the right, not far from Piazza Barberini, one comes to the 17th century Church of **Santa Maria della Concezione**, containing works by Guido Reni and Domenichino. In the underground chapels the walls are decorated with the bones of Capucin monks. Next comes the **Church of Sant'Isidoro**, with paintings by Maratta, and then **Palazzo Margherita**, formerly the residence of Queen Margherita.

At the top is the Porta Pinciana.

From Piazza Venezia, Via Cesare Battisti leads to Piazza dei SS. Apostoli, which takes its name from the **Basilica of SS. Apostoli**, adjoining Palazzo Colonna. The Church was built in the 6th century, but was many times restored, and completely rebuilt by Fontana and Valadier. The interesting interior contains several valuable works of art.

Through the narrow alleyways at the side of the square, by way of Via San Marcello and Via delle Muratte, one reaches the famous **Trevi Fountain**, which ranks as one of the most beautiful fountains in Rome and one of best known in the world, owing to the somptuousness of its decorative elements which merge with the structural elements, the spirited spatial solutions, and the bold, and at the same time monumental, rhythm of the architecture.

It was built for Pope Clement XII. The water of the Fountain was called "Virgin", because its source was indicated to the soldiers of Agrippa by a young girl; Agrippa then had the water conveyed to Rome in 19 B.C. The Fountain was built in the middle of the 18th century by the architect Salvi. The large central niche is carved out of one side of the palace of the Dukes of Poli, and is filled with the statue of the god Neptune drawn in a chariot by two Tritons. The sculptures are by Bracci. Popular tradition has it that those who wish to return to Rome must throw a small coin into the basin before they leave.

VIA VENETO

The Fountain of Trevi, near Via del Corso, is so called after the term « trivio », or cross-roads or exactly the place where three roads meet. The construction of the majestic marble set, of great scenographic effect, was begun under the Pope Clement XII and completed in 1762. The project was of the architect Salvi (1697-1751). In the centre, the mythological figure of Ocean on a chariot carried by two marine horses guided by Triton. Thronged with tourists all the year long, it is considered one of the most beautiful fountains in the world. The palace on its background is that of the Dukes of Poli.

Piazza di Spagna,
one of the best known squares of Rome, colourful and fascinating, the gathering point for foreigners, artists and young people. For many years, nothing has changed here, nothing has lost its charm. The best known, most fashionable streets of Rome start from here, such as Via Condotti with the famous Café Greco, which dates from the 18th century and became the centre of Rome's intellectual life; the fashionable, crowded Via Frattina; Via del Babuino, well known for its many private art galleries, where all the year round one may visit shows of Italian and foreign artists; the celebrated Via Margutta, the favourite place for artists' studios and exhibitions.

On one side of Piazza di Spagna stands the **Palazzo della Propaganda Fide**, the work partly of Bernini and partly of Borromini; the work of the latter is above all to be seen in the lateral façade with its bizarre and restless technique.

In the centre of the square, right opposite the fine Spanish Steps, is the famous **Fontana della Barcaccia**, designed by Pietro Bernini (father of the great Bernini), perhaps with the help of his son.

The finest and best known feature of the square however, is the great stairway called the **Spanish Steps**, which, by a succession of flights and landings, leads up to the **Church of Trinità dei Monti**. In spring, the whole staircase is gay with the flowers of the stall holders, who have long since replaced the artist's models, who used to come here in their free time to sell bunches of violets.

In May, a beautiful display of azaleas is held here.

The staircase was planned by Francesco De Sanctis at the beginning of the 18th century.

At the top of the steps are the **Piazza** and **Church of Trinità dei Monti**. The Church is a French one, dating from the 16th century, with a staircase by Fontana in front, and a fine façade by Maderno. In the interior are interesting works of art.

The Spanish Steps lead up to the **Pincio**, another of the Roman hills, and certainly one of the most beautiful and romantic.

First, along the Via Trinità dei Monti, one comes to the 16th century **Villa Medici**. It houses the **French Academy**, which gives hospitality to young French artists who wish to advance their artistic studies. The Villa contains many very interesting pieces of classical sculpture, including the famous "Head of Meleager"

From here one enters the **Pincio**, a lovely public park where one can enjoy some of the most attractive walks in Rome, thanks to the fine views and the wonderful sunsets to be seen from here. The park was designed by Valadier at the beginning of the 19th century; it is crossed by a number of avenues, all of which are very attractive. One of these, the Avenue of the Magnolias, leads to **Villa Borghese**, another lovely Roman park, and also the largest.

VIA CONDOTTI BY NIGHT

THE STEPS AND THE CHURCH
OF TRINITA' DEI MONTI ➤

A VIEW OF PIAZZA DEL POPOLO FROM THE VILLA BORGHESE VILLA BORGHESE

BORGHESE GALLERY

It was planned by Cardinal Scipio Borghese, who had a large stretch of land, planted with vineyards, made into a park to surround the Casino Borghese (specially built by the Cardinal to house a Museum).

The whole park is full of beautiful and romantic prospects, which serve as a setting for the **Casino Borghese** mentioned above. As has already been said, the Casino is one of the few examples of buildings designed specially to house very important paintings and sculptures, so as to create a Gallery and Art Museum of a well-defined character. It was planned by Cardinal Scipio Borghese, who entrusted its construction to Van Santen (Vasanzio), who completed it in 1616. The Cardinal then began to collect great masterpieces, and his enterprise was continued by his successors with the same critical acumen. The Gallery, which now belongs to the Nation, houses one of the most important collections of Italian art, particularly of the 17th and 18th centuries and has the merit of quite exceptional consistency.

Among the most important works we would mention: "Paolina Bonaparte" by Canova, "David", "Apollo and Daphne", and "The Rape of Proserpine", all by Bernini; "The Deposition" by Raphael; "Leda with the Swan" by Sodoma; "Youth with a Basket of Fruit" by Caravaggio; "The Virgin of the Palafrenieri", "David", "The young Bacchus ill", and "St. Jerome", all by Caravaggio, and "Sacred and profane Love" by Titian. There are also works by Rubens, Antonello da Messina, D. Dossi and Giorgione.

THE BORGHESE GALLERY

◄ GALLERY OF THE EMPERORS   PAULINE BORGHESE (Canova)

DAVID (Bernini)

APOLLO AND DAPHNE (Bernini)

THE ENTOBMENT (Rubens)

Near the Borghese Gallery are the large **Zoological Gardens** with the **Zoological Museum**.

The **African Museum** in the Via Aldovrandi nearby, of great ethnological and historical interest, is worth visiting.

Via Aldovrandi leads to **Valle Giulia** with the very interesting **National Gallery of Modern Art,** containing a vast and representative collection of works of art from Italy and other countries, starting from neoclassicism and continuing up to the latest trends of contemporary art. Series of lectures, study courses, important cultural manifestations and shows of the works of great exponents of contemporary art are often held in the Gallery.

It is not possible here to give a comprehensive list of the works of art, the artists, and the trends reprensented in this Gallery. Suffice it to mention only the names of Cànova, Hayez, Fattori, Signorini, Gemito, De Chirico, Carrà, Campigli, Mario and Raphael Mafai, Sassu and Guttuso.

Likewise in Valle Giulia, one comes to **Villa Giulia**, which houses the **National Museum of Villa Giulia**, a most impressive museum with a vast collection of works of art of the pre-Roman period, from Latium, Umbria and Etruria. The collection is distributed over thirty rooms, and as it is impossible to mention here even the most important works, we will only say that the famous "Apollo of Veii" and the "Sarcophagus of the Bride and Bridegroom", two marvellous Etruscan works, are displayed here.

From Viale delle Belle Arti one comes to the crossing of Via Flaminia, or one can return the way one came to Villa Borghese.

The Via del Corso, which runs from Piazza Venezia to Piazza del Popolo, is Rome's most central and most important street. On either side of it are many palaces from various periods which bear testimony to its long history.

The first of these, on the left, is the 17th century **Palazzo Bonaparte**, and then on the right comes the **Palazzo Salviati** (n. 271), and **Palazzo Odescalchi** (n. 260).

On the left, the elegant **Palazzo Doria**, which has been altered several times, now presents a fine rococo façade. It contains the **Doria Pamphili Gallery**, one of the best private collections in Rome. Only a few of its many masterpieces will be mentioned here: "Mary Magdalene" and "The Flight into Egypt" by Caravaggio, "Portrait of Pope Innocent X", by Velasquez, and works by Rubens, Bernini, Lotto, Titian, Dossi, Bassano, Parmigianino, Correggio, Tintoretto, Preti, Guercino, and other famous artists.

Attached to the palace is the **Church of Santa Maria in Via Lata**, with a fine façade by Pietro da Cortona, and then, in Piazza del Collegio Romano, the **National Library**, housed in the fine Collegio Romano, a 16th century building by Ammannati.

Returning to the Corso, one finds the **Church of San Marcello**, by Sansovino with a façade by Fontana, a masterpiece of baroque art.

Further on, by way of Via del Caravita, one comes to the **Church of Sant'Ignazio**, surrounded by fine 18th century houses. It was designed by the Jesuit Grassi in a somewhat florid and theatrical baroque style. Most of the interior owes its decoration to Andrea Pozzo, a passionate student of bold, spectacular and luminous perspectives.

Returning to the Corso, one takes on the left, Via di Pietra, which leads to the remains of the **Temple of Neptune** (actually, it was the Temple of Hadrian), with some very elegant Corinthian columns still standing.

Then one arrives at **Piazza Colonna**, so called after the tall **Column of Marcus Aurelius**, dating from the 2nd century A.D. In style it resembles Trajan's Column, but its workmanship is more decadent and the rhythm of its components is weak.

The 16th century Fountain is by Della Porta.

The square is surrounded by fine 16th and 18th century houses.

Next one comes to Piazza Montecitorio, where stands the **Palazzo di Montecitorio** (now the seat of the Chamber of Deputies), which was built initially to the plan of Bernini, and completed by Fontana.

From Piazza Colonna one continues along Via del Corso, passing the **Church of Santa Maria in Via** with a fine baroque façade by Rainaldi, and then the **Café Aragno**, once a famous meeting place for intellectuals and politicians.

Not far from it, in the Piazza di San Lorenzo in Lucina, stands the **Church of San Lorenzo in Lucina**, of very ancient origin, but rebuilt in the Middle Ages; the portico and campanile, still intact, date from that period. The rest is baroque, especially the richly decorated interior. There are also works by Guido Reni and Bernini, as well as the grid on which St. Lawrence was martyred.

Passing **Palazzo Ruspoli**, built by Ammannati, one arrives at the **Church of San Carlo**, built by Longhi in the 17th century, whereas the very slender dome is by Pietro da Cortona. In the richly decorated interior a fine work by Maratta.

The Corso ends in the magnificent **Piazza del Popolo**, designed by Valadier, a great town-planner of the late 18th and early 19th centuries; he had the idea of connecting it, by means of two large semicircles, with the Pincio (also designed by him, as already mentioned), thus creating a large open space without any rhetorical overstatement. The square had previously undergone an important architectural transformation in the 17th century, Carlo Rainaldi had planned the two **Churches of Santa Maria di Monte Santo and Santa Maria dei Miracoli**, at the junction of the three important thoroughfares — Via del Babuino, Via del Corso and Via di Ripetta. The exterior of these two churches is the work of Bernini; the interior of the first is by Rainaldi and Bernini, that of the second by Fontana. In this way, Piazza del Popolo has become a very harmonious whole, of generous proportions and above all, well related in its parts.

In the centre of the square stands the **Obelisk of Flaminius**, an Egyptian work of the second millenium B.C., brought to Rome at the time of Augustus. At the end of the square is the **Church of Santa Maria del Popolo**, built in the Middle Ages, but several times rebuilt, until it was given its final appearance at the time of the Renaissance.

The façade is in the Renaissance style, as is also the interior, although partly modified by later decorations. It contains valuable works by Pinturicchio (who painted all the frescoes in the first chapel of the right aisle), Bregno, Sebastiano del Piombo, Bernini, Sansovino (with his splendid funerary monuments and Caravaggio (here represented by the two masterpieces "The Conversion of St. Paul", and "The crucifixion of St. Peter"). It should also be noted that the whole apse is built to the design of Bramante, while the Chigi Chapel was planned by Raphael.

Finnally one leaves Piazza del Popolo by **Porta del Popolo**, the combined work of Bernini, Vignola, and perhaps even Michelangelo. From this Gate starts the Via Flaminia, a very important thoroughfare of ancient Rome, which connected the city with Rimini. Beyond the Gate opens the Piazzale Flaminio, with the main entrance to the park of Villa Borghese.

Continuing along Via Flaminia, one reaches, a little beyond the Viale delle Belle Arti, the **Palazzina of Pius IV**, perhaps the work of Ammannati, and still further on, there is Vignola's elegant **"Tempietto di Sant'Andrea"** (16th century).

This is the quarter where modern sports installations have been provided, the adjacent Viale Tiziano leads to the **Flaminian Stadium**, built by the architect Nervi, with adjoining sports and training grounds, as well as a covered swimming pool and other facilities for various sports.

Nearby is also the large, fashionable quarter of Parioli. The Viale di Parioli leads to **Acqua Acetosa**, a mineral spring.

If, however, one wishes to continue along Via Flaminia, one can reach **Ponte Milvio**, an ancient Roman bridge, much restored, Beyond the bridge, lies the **Foro italico**, a large and perfectly equipped centre with important sports installations, including the huge Olympic Stadium of the Statues, the swimming pools, and the well laid out tennis courts, accommodating many players. The slopes of Monte Mario dominate the Foro Italico.

From Piazza Venezia one goes along the Via del Corso and then takes Via Lata on the left, to reach Piazza del Collegio Romano; from here, by way of Via Piè di Marmo, one arrives at Piazza Minerva with Bernini's **Elephant** in the centre. Here stands the **Church of Santa Maria sopra Minerva**. In spite of the frequent alterations it suffered in the Renaissance and baroque period, the Church still preserves fundamentally its origin Gothic style, and is the only example of a Gothic church in Rome. Its Gothic character is most evident in the interior.

The large number of chapels all around the Church are full of works of art. Only the most important can be mentioned here: the funerary monuments in the 6th chapel of the right aisle, by Della Porta; the Caraffa Chapel in the right transept, adorned with beautiful fresco paintings by Filippo Lippi and a tomb by Giovanni Cosma; the very fine "Risen Christ" by Michelangelo on the left pilaster of the Presbytery; the funerary monuments by Antonio da Sangallo behind the high altar; the Tomb of Pietro Bembo, on the floor of the Presbytery; the fine funerary monument by Bernini in the left aisle, and "San Sebastian", a statue by Tino da Caima-

no in the third chapel. Mention should also be made of works by Sansovino, Pinturicchio, Melozzo da Forlì, Baccio Bandinelli, Rainaldi, and others.

From Piazza Minerva one proceeds to the nearby Piazza della Rotonda, where stands the **Pantheon**, one of the most famous monuments of Roman art. The name indicates that this was a temple dedicated to all the gods. It was built by Marcus Agrippa, as can be seen from the inscription on the entablature outside, but altered at the time of Hadrian. It is an example of Roman art in the Hellenistic style, with a genuine sense of classical architecture, as can be seen in the various architectural features and in the spirit which pervades the whole building. The outside is seen as a large circular mass, with a pronaos in front, resting on columns and surmounted by a large gable. The inside is circular in form with a dome, thus creating a clear, spherical space, at once confined and majestic. The interior receives light through a single aperture in the centre of the dome ephasizing the coffered decoration and above all creating a luminous effect which stresses the harmonious blending of all the parts.

In Christian times, the Pantheon was turned into a church, which undoubtedly accounts for its excellent state of preservation down to our own time. A number of works of art are to be found in the chapels inside, and in addition the tombs of important personalities of Italian history and art, among them that of Raphael.

The Pantheon, in the historical centre of the City, is one of the best kept ancient monuments in the world. So called because it was a temple dedicated to many deities, particularly to Mars and Venus, it was built by order of the consul Agrippa, friend and son-in-law of Augustus, in 27 BC. Surprisingly, almost all we can admire today of this famous monument, goes back to Roman times, even the dome and the massive bronze door of the entrance, which goes back to Hadrian's time (76-138 AD), the emperor who had it re-built in 130 AD. In 609 the building became a Christian church and this probably contributed to its preservation, as in other similar cases. In the interior, where once there were the statues of various gods, there are some tombs, among which those of King Victor Emmanuel II, Humbert I and the Queen Margharet and Raphael Sanzio, the famous painter.

A PLASTIC MODEL OF ROME BY I. GISMONDI - THE PANTHEON - RECONSTRUCTION

On leaving the Pantheon, one takes Via Giustiniani to arrive at the **Church of San Luigi dei Francesi**, a 16th century building showing the hand of Fontana, and, in the façade, that of Della Porta. Inside are three magnificent masterpieces by Caravaggio: "St. Matthew with the Angel", "The Calling of St. Matthew" and "The Martyrdom of St. Matthew". Mention should also be made of the frescoes by Dominichino in the second chapel on the right, with scenes from the "Life of Santa Cecilia".

By way of Via San Salvatore and then Via del Rinascimento, one reaches Piazza Madama, called after **Palazzo Madama** (now the seat of the Italian Senate). It has a majestic baroque façade, designed by Cigoli and Marucelli. In the interior it contains the large hall where the Senate meets and also a well-stocked Library.

A little further on, one comes to the 16th century **Palazzo della Sapienza** which at present houses the State Archives (it was formerly the seat of the University). The inner Courtyard, designed by Della Porta in an austere Renaissance style, is particularly interesting. Above it rises the **Chapel of Sant'Ivo della Sapienza**, one of Borromini's most fascinating and original

creations, marked by the projection and re-entry of the architectural masses which seem to expand and lose their shape under the artist's hands, in order finally to recede with a sudden, spiral movement into the lantern. This is one of the finest examples of Borromini's art, which, though essentially baroque, yet seems to go back to the ardour and mysticism of Gothic forms. The same dynamic curving lines are repeated in the interior of the chapel.

Next, by way of Via dei Canestrari, one comes to **Piazza Navona**, another very important centre of Rome, with its wealth of history and art. The shape of the square recalls that of a stadium, and in effect it was built over the Stadium of Domitian which stood there before. Three fountains adorn the square, the one in the middle is Bernini's famous **Fountain of the Four Rivers**. The project was entrusted to him only after long hesitation, and only when Pope Innocent X got to know of the artist's design by indirect means; up to that time, he had been opposed to him. The fountain forms a completely harmonious whole of sculpture, architecture, and one might almost say, even of painting, in view of the painterly effects it achieves. The four

INTERIOR OF THE PANTHEON

main rivers of the world are depicted here (the Nile, the Ganges, the Danube and the River Plate), respectively representing the four continents under the authority of the Pope. In the centre rises an obelisk.

One should also note the **Fountain of the Moor**, designed by Bernini, but executed by Mari, and the **Fountain of Neptune**, designed by Della Porta, but completed only at a later date.

The square is surrounded by interesting buildings,

NAVONA SQUARE

bearing witness to a period of exceptional importance for Rome, that of the two great artists, Bernini and Borromini, two outstanding masters whose creative genius left a profound mark; they often quarelled with each other, partly because of the varying support of the Popes, but in spite of this they left the mark of their originality upon the whole art of the period.

Thus it was that, right in front of Bernini's fountain, was built Borromini's beautiful **Church of Sant'Agnese in Agone**, with its concave façade, characteristic of the master's style.

Also in the square, one finds the **Palazzo Pamphili** by Rainaldi and the **Chiesa del Sacro Cuore di Maria**, in the Renaissance style. Near the Church of Sant'Agnese is Via dell'Anima, which leads to the **Church of Santa Maria dell'Anima**, the façade of which may perhaps be the work of Sangallo, and the Campanile by Bramante. In any case, it is a good example of Renaissance architecture, which in the interior shows the influence of German art (in fact, the Church belongs to the German community). Interesting works of art are to be seen in the interior.

From Piazza Venezia one takes Via del Plebiscito and Corso Vittorio Emanuele as far as Largo Argentina, and from there one proceeds along Via Arenula to Ponte Garibaldi, which one crosses in order to arrive at the quarter most characteristic of the true Roman population — **Trastevere**.

After crossing the bridge, one immediately reaches Piazza Sonnino, in which stands a monument to the Roman dialect poet Gioacchino Belli, and a 13th century tower. A little further on is the **Church of San Crisogono**, which underwent numerous restorations that have entirely changed its original Early Christian and Romanesque architecture. The interior in particular has a rich stucco decoration, while the ground plan has remained unchanged, as well as the beautiful columns dividing the aisles. One should also note a fine mosaic by Cavallini and frescoes dating from the 9th century.

On entering Viale Trastevere, one turns to the left into Via Genovesi, where stands the **Church of San Giovanni Battista dei Genovesi**, with a fine 15th century cloister. Then, by Via di Santa Cecilia, one comes to the **Church of Santa Cecilia**. This church, too, has lost

94

S. MARIA'S CHURCH IN TRASTEVERE

its original structure, and has today an 18th century façade with a portico by Fuga. The campanile, in the other hand, is Romanesque. The interior has a decidedly 18th century atmosphere, which has completely changed its appearance. Among the works of art that merit attention are: the famous statue of Santa Cecilia, one of Maderno's finest creations and a superb Canopy by Arnolfo di Cambio; moreover, in the basement, there are particularly interesting remains of buildings prior to the church, which go back right to the period of the Roman Republic. Adjoining the church there is a monastery with a fine fresco by Cavallini (13th century).

One returns to Viale Trastevere and takes Via San Francesco Ripa, which leads to the Piazza where stands the **Basilica of Santa Maria in Trastevere**, one of the earliest, if not the earliest, founded at Rome (3rd century). In spite of many alterations, it still retains its original structure, and what is more, the spirit that animated this ancient building almost intact. The façade, apart from the portico, dates from the 12th century, as does the campanile; the façade is adorned with mosaics of the period. The interior also has largely preserved

its original appearance, mainly owing to mosaics of the period (12th - 13th centuries). One might single out for mention those by Cavallini, and above all, those in the apse.

By way of Via della Scala, to the right of the Church, one reaches the **Church of Santa Maria della Scala**, and then, by Via Lungara, one comes to **Palazzo Corsini**, by Fuga (18th century), today the seat of the **National Academy of Ancient Art**, containing some very interesting works: "The Virgin" by Murillo; "Venetian Landscapes" by Canaletto; "St. John the Baptist" by Caravaggio, as well as works by Van Dyck, Rubens, Preti, Saraceni, Gentileschi, Piazzetta, Baciccia, Sustermans, Maratta, and others.

This palace is also the seat of the **Accademia dei Lincei** and contains the **Odescalchi Collection of Armour.**

Opposite, is the entrance to the Farnesina, another of Baldassare Peruzzi's masterpieces, conceived in a clear Renaissance style. It was the sumptuous residence of the Chigi family; at present it is used for official occasions of the Accademia dei Lincei. The Farnesina was adorned with frescoes and decorated by outstand-

ing artists; such as Raphael, Sebastiano da Piombo and Peruzzi, the work here being some of their best.

The Farnesina also contains the **National Collection of Engravings**, which is particularly rich and interesting.

On the left of Via della Lungara is **Palazzo Salviati**.

The road ends at the Porta di Santo Spirito, built by Sangallo, and nearby is the **Church of Sant'Onofrio** (15th century), where Torquato Tasso died. In the adjoining Monastery, the **Tasso Museum** has been installed. Inside the Church are works by Peruzzi and Boltraffio.

Above the church rises the **Janiculum**, one of the most attractive places on the outskirts of Rome, another of the hills on which Rome stands. On the way, one meets various monuments, including the one erected to Garibaldi, who organised there the defence of the Republic of Rome. The **Ossuary of the Janiculum** is dedicated to the soldiers of Garibaldi who fell in this

THE MONUMENT TO GIUSEPPE GARIBALDI

THE TIBER WITH PETER'S AND CASTEL SANT'ANGELO

battle.

Near at hand is the **Villa Pamphili**, a fine building by Algardi. It is surrounded by a huge park (the largest in Rome), and is one of the most attractive and romantic places of the city.

Next to it are the **Catacombs of San Pancrazio** and the ancient **Basilica di San Pancrazio**.

The interesting walk around the Janiculum ends at Porta Settimiana, whence one returns to the Tiber bank. At Ponte Vittorio Emanuele one takes Lungotevere Sant'Angelo, which leads to the massive building of **Castel Sant'Angelo**, also known as the Mausoleum of Hadrian. It dates from the imperial period, the second century A.D., and was to serve as the tomb of the Emperor Hadrian. The Emperor Aurelian had it made into a fortress and connected to the walls built by him for the defence of the city.

Castel Sant'Angelo has always been closely con-

nected with the history of Rome; many important personalities were imprisoned here, and it served as a place of refuge for Popes and rulers. Only in this century has it been completely restored, and it now houses a **Museum** with collections of armour and documents referring to the history of the Castle itself, its construction and its restorations. All the rooms can be visited, from the prison to the Papal apartments and the many fine halls with their beautiful decorations, all of them connected with noteworthy historical events or important figures.

Behind the Castle stands the **Casa dei Mutilati** a 20th century building, the interior of which is adorned with sculptures and paintings by contemporary artists.

Lastly, one reaches the monumental **Palace of Justice** (Law Courts), built by the architect Calderini. From the Piazza Cavour behind it, one can take the road to Monte Mario.

CASTEL SANT'ANGELO
The Courtyard of the Angel

CASTEL SANT'ANGELO

THE VATICAN CITY

The Vatican State, one of the smallest in the world, is unique in that it is the spiritual centre of the Roman Catholic religion. It emerged as an autonomous State, independent of Italy, on Febraury 11, 1929, as the result of the conclusion of the Lateran Pact. Its history, however, goes back to the Emperor Constantine, who wished the first great early Christian Basilica to be built on the spot where St. Peter met his death, and where so many Christians had been persecuted. From that time, events connected with the Vatican are closely bound up with the history of the Papacy.

THE BUILDING OF ST. PETER'S

The history of the present Basilica begins in 1506, the year in which work was begun on Bramante's plan, which was substantially adhered to, in spite of many alterations. The site was previously occupied by the great early Christian church of the 4th century, erected by Constantine.

Bramante's work was soon interrupted, and his plan was to some extent modified in 1547, by that of Michelangelo, of which the apse and the dome now remain (although the dome has been made higher). In 1606 Maderno took over the work, transforming, at the Pope's order, the ground plan of a Greek cross to that of a Latin cross, and altering the lines of the façade. In 1657, Bernini completed the building with his creation of the majestic Colonnade of St. Peter's Square.

Piazza San Pietro is surrounded by this vast Colonnade in the form of an ellipse, the two arms of which diverge near the façade, which is thus given a new perspective. In the centre of the square stands an Egyptian **Obelisk,** taken from Nero's Circus, crowned with a cross. There are two **Fountains**, one on either side, one by Maderno, the other by Bernini.

RECONCILIATION STREET   ST. PETER'S SQUARE AND BASILICA ➤

THE BASILICA OF ST. PETER: The Façade

There is a great flight of stairs in front of the Church, and then the façade rises with its powerful architectural development. As seen today, it is the work of Maderno. It consists of an order of columns projecting from the masonry, with a pronounced cornice above, in the centre of which is carved the name of Pope Paul V, who commissioned the work from Maderno, Between the columns are windows, the largest of which, the one in the centre, is the **Loggia of the Benedictions**. It is here that the Pope appears to impart his blessing "Urbi et Orbi" to the faithful gathered in the square.

The Interior

Through the entrances along the front one steps into the VESTIBULE, the ancient "endonarthex" of the early Christian basilicas. It too is the work of Maderno, and is decorated with stuccos and mosaics. Among the latter, the one by Giotto, depicting "La Navicella" above the main entrance, is particularly interesting. There is also a fine work by Bernini in the portico: the "Equestrian Statue of the Emperor Constantine". The two famous doors should also be noted; the **Bronze Door** on the left, which formed part of the Old St. Peter's and is divided into sculptured panels, and the **Holy Door** which is opened only during Holy Years.

One now enters the Church, which is the largest in the world; indeed, the visitor immediately gets the impression of majesty and grandeur, not only owing to its exceptional dimensions, but above all owing to the whole effect of the architectural and decorative elements.

ST. PETER'S BASILICA - Interior   ST. PETER'S CHAIR (Bernini) ➤

INTERIOR OF ST. PETER'S DOME

The Church, which seems to have three aisles, has really only one, with intercommunicating side chapels. The design is due to Maderno and Bernini.

Only a brief indication will be given here of some of the major works of art it contains:

Chapels on the right:

Chapel of the Pietà: "Pietà" by Michelangelo, one of his most famous works.

Chapel of the Relics: "Crucifix", probably by Cavallini.

Chapel of St. Sebastiano: "Martyrdom of St. Sebastian", by Domenichino.

Tomb of Countess Matilda of Canossa, by Bernini.

Chapel of the Blessed Sacrament: Canopy, by Bernini.

Chapel of Gregory XIII: Fresco depicting "Our Lady

104

LA PIETA' OF MICHELANGELO

of Succour", (12th century).

Right Transept

Altar of the "Navicella": Copy of Giotto's Mosaic of the "Navicella".

Chapel of St. Michael: "St. Michael the Archangel", by Guido Reni.

Apse

This contains the imposing **Chair of St. Peter**, an outstanding work by Bernini. It is a solemn, luminous creation, in which the artist's imagination has been given free rein, achieving magnificent effects, without ever lapsing into exaggeration and pretentiousness.

Altogether, the Chair is, as it were, a solemn hymn to the relic it encloses (the wooden chair which, according to tradition, belonged to St. Peter), and to the place where it stands, thus forming a marvellous conclusion to the Basilica.

Next one should note the **Dome**, which is about 120 metres high, up to the lantern. Below it stands the **Bronze Canopy**, supported by four magnificent twisted columns, likewise by Bernini.

Left Transept

Altar of St. Peter's Crucifixion: a mosaic of this subject, after Guido Reni's painting.

Chapels on the left

Above all, the **Sacristy** should be visited, and the famous **Treasure of St. Peter's**, kept in the Treasury, consisting of a wealth of items and jewels of incalculable value, the gift of thousands of worshippers.

One now returns to the Church.

BASILICA OF ST. PETER'S - The Vatican Catacombs - Tomb of Saint Peter

THE PAOLINA CHAPEL - Interior

Clementine Chapel: Monument to Pius VII, by Thorwaldsen.

Choir Chapel: Baroque Organ.

Chapel of the Presentation: Mosaic on this subject, after a painting by Romanelli.

Baptistery: the fine Font is by Fontana.

In order to ascend Michelangelo's **Dome**, one takes a door inside the church, near the Monument to Maria Clementina Sobiesky. From the Dome, one gets a fine view of the interior of the Church, but above all one enjoys a wonderful view over Rome.

It is also interesting to visit the **Vatican Grottos**, which stretch under the Basilica and the adjoining areas. They contain sarcophagi from the previous Basilica as well as tombs dating from the Roman times. Here too, the **Tomb of St. Peter** has been discovered, in the exact spot indicated by tradition.

The entrance to the Vatican Grottos is in Largo Braschi.

THE VATICAN PALACE

The Vatican Palace consists of a large group of buildings, a few of which serve as the residence of the Pope and the Pontifical Court, while most of them house Museums, Galleries, Libraries and Archives. These buildings have a very long history, and in the course of centuries, under the patronage of various Popes, they have undergone a continuous series of enlargements and embellishments, entrusted to the most celebrated artists of the time.

Only some parts of the **"Apostolic Pontifical Palace"** can be visited, and these only on the occasion of general and private audiences with the Holy Father. On such occasions, one enters by the **Bronze Door**, goes up Bernini's superb **Scala Regia** and enters the **Sala Regia** (the work of Sangallo) and the **Cappella Paolina** (this cannot always be visited). In it are Michelangelo's famous frescoes of the "Conversion of St. Paul" and the "Crucifixion of St. Peter".

Another staircase, the **Scala Papale**, leads to the **Sala Clementina** which gives access to the Pope's study.

THE VATICAN MUSEUMS

In order to reach the entrance to the Vatican

VATICAN PICTURE GALLERY - The Deposition (Caravaggio)

◄ VATICAN PICTURE GALLERY-The Virgin Mary of Foligno (Raffaello)

THE VATICAN LIBRARY

Museums, one starts from the right hand Colonnade of St. Peter's Square, and takes Via di Porta Angelica which one follows as far as Piazza del Risorgimento. Then, by way of Via Leone IV and Viale del Vaticano, one arrives at the entrance of the Museums.

The first nucleus of these Museums took shape at the time of the Renaissance, and was housed in the Palazzetto del Belvedere. After the reign of Pope Julius II, who collected mainly classical sculptures, other Popes continued and completed this work of choosing and collecting the greatest art treasures.

Only brief indications will be given here of the Museums and Galleries and the things they contain. First one enters a **Vestibule,** from which starts a **Spiral Staircase** (20th century), which leads to the various floors.

THE VATICAN PICTURE GALLERY

The Statue in the Vestibule is dedicated to Pius XI,

the founder of the Gallery. It occupies 15 rooms, each devoted to a single artist or school.

Room 1: works of the early centuries of the Christian era, and of Byzantine artists. A fine "Last Judgment" of the 11th century should be noted.

Room 2: Giotto and his school. The "Stefaneschi" triptych is by Giotto. Also of interest are the "Stories of St. Stephen" by A. Lorenzetti, and the "Annunciation" by Giovanni di Paolo.

Room 3: Fra Angelico. We mention "The Virgin with Saints", and "Scenes from the Life of St. Nicholas of Bari", by the master. There are also works by Gentile da Fabriano, B. Gozzoli and F. Lippi.

Room 4: Melozzo da Forlì is represented here with "The Nomination of Platina" and some "Angels making Music".

Room 5: Minor 15th century painters.
Room 6: Works by Crivelli (2nd half of 15th century).
Room 7: Umbrian painters of the 15th century. Works by Perugino and Pinturicchio.

111

Room 8: Raphael ("Coronation of the Virgin", "Madonna of Foligno", and "The Transfiguration").

Room 9: Leonardo da Vinci with is beautiful "St. Jerome".

Room 10: Venetian artists of the 16th century. Titian: "The Madonna of San Niccolò dei Frari"; Veronese: "St. Helen", An Allegorical Painting.

Room 11: artists of the 16th century and of the early baroque period (Barocci, Vasari, Carracci).

Room 12: artists of the 17th century. Domenichino: "Communion of St. Jerome"; Caravaggio: "Deposition".

Room 13: 17th and 18th centuries: Maratta, Gentileschi, Murillo, Pietro da Cortona, Van Dyck ("Francesco Saverio").

Room 14: 17th and 18 centuries: Rubens: "Apotheosis of Vincenzo Gonzaga".

Room 15: The Portrait Room, containing fine portraits by outstanding artists.

Next to the Picture Gallery is the **Museum of Contemporary Art**, with works by Soffici, De Pisis, Carrà, De Chirico, Sironi, and others.

Now comes the group of Museums of Sculpture, the first of which is the MUSEO PIO CLEMENTINO, with a series of rooms containing a vast collection of statues, sarcophagi and mosaics of Greek and Roman times. Among the more important pieces are the following: **"Laocoon"**, the famous Greek sculpture of the first century B.C.; a copy of the **"Apollo Sauroctonos"**, by Praxiteles, and a copy of the **"Hermes"** by the same sculptor; the **"Belvedere Apollo"**, copy of a 4th century Greek original; the **"Apoxyomenos"**, another famous sculpture by Lysippus (a copy); the **"Belvedere Torso"**, a statue of great artistic value for the close anatomical detail and its intense vitality.

Next comes the MUSEO CHIARAMONTI, likewise rich in statues, sarcophagi, bas-reliefs and busts. It has various sections, one of which, the **Braccio Nuovo**, contains some excellent pieces, such as the **"Augustus of Prima Porta"**, a **"Figure of the Nile"**, and a few copies of Greek statues.

Next one enters the VATICAN LIBRARY, which contains one of the most valuable book collections in the world, both for number, rarity and importance.

It occupies a series of rooms, all with rich decorations, mostly by De Angelis.

To mention only a few of the most important pieces: a **"Vatican Codex of the Bible"** dating from the 4th century; a **"Divine Comedy"** with illustrations by Botticelli: the priceless **"Book of Hours"** with exquisite miniatures.

There follow the **Gallery of Urban VIII** (with a collection of scientific instruments), the **Museo Sacro**, (containing all the "Sancta Sanctorum" i.e. all sacred objects), the **Sala delle Nozze Aldobrandine**, the **Chapel of Pope Pius V**, and the **Room of the Sacred Vestments.**

THE BORGIA APARTMENT is a suite of 6 rooms, in which Pope Alexander VI used to live. It is particularly noteworthy, because it was for the most part decorated by Pinturicchio.

Room 1, called the Room of the Sibyls, because of the **"12 Sibyls"** and **"12 Apostles"** "12 Prophets" depicted in the lunettes.

Room 2, called the **Room of the Creed** from the paintings of the Apostles and Prophets who propagated the Christian Creed.

Room 3, with paintings depicting the **"Liberal Arts"**, by Antonio da Viterbo.

Room 4, entirely decorated by Pinturicchio with **"Scenes from the Life of St. Catherine"**, and **"Scenes from the Lives of other Saints"**.

Room 5, decorated with **"Scenes from the Life of Christ"**.

Room 6, This once contained the portraits of many Popes.

From the Borgia Apartment one returns to Room 5 of the Museo Sacro, and thence, by way of a corridor, one reaches the

SISTINE CHAPEL

This is one of the most outstanding masterpieces of Italian art. The Chapel is called after Sixtus IV, the Pope for whom it was built by the architect Giovannino de' Dolci. The Conclaves and particularly solemn ceremonies are held here.

The Chapel, which is celebrated for Michelangelo's frescoes, has on its walls panels with pictures by equally famous painters. Starting from the altar and following the right hand wall, one sees

Panel 1 - **"Moses on the way to Egypt"**, by Pinturicchio and Perugino.

Panel 2 - **"Moses and the Daughter of Jethro"**, by Botticelli.

Panel 3 - **"The Crossing of the Red Sea"**, by Cosimo Rosselli.

Panel 4 - **"Scenes from the Life of Moses"**, by Rosselli.

Panel 5 - **"The Punishment of Korah"**, by Botticelli.

Panel 6 - **"The Death of Moses"**, by Signorelli.

Returning to the altar, one now looks at the left wall:

Panel 1 - **"The Baptism of Christ"**, by Pinturicchio or Perugino.

Panel 2 - **"The Temptation of Christ"**, by Botticelli.

Panel 3 - **"The Calling of the Apostles"**, by Ghirlandaio.

Panel 4 - **"The Sermon on the Mount"**, by Rosselli.

Panel 5 - **"Christ giving the Keys to St. Peter"**, by Perugino.

Panel 6 - **"The Last Supper"**, by Rosselli.

Now to take a look at Michelangelo's great masterpieces.

On the great wall of the altar is depicted the **"Last Judgment"**, painted between 1536 and 1545, after he had already painted the entire vault of the Chapel. It is a majestic representation of the last day of Judgment: the centre is dominated by the figure of Christ the Judge, who with His raised arm, seems to give a whirling movement to the whole scene. All the figures in this huge fresco seem to be immersed in an apocalyptic gloom, pervaded by the drama of life and death.

The frescoes that decorate the vault, which were painted between 1508 and 1512, are another magnificent achievement. Michelangelo's architectural disposition of the space serves as a setting for his scenes and figures, and to divide the whole in a rational manner.

THE SISTINA CHAPEL (Michelangelo) ➤

THE SISTINA CHAPEL- The last Judgement (Michelangelo)   The Vault of the Chapel (Michelangelo) ➤

◄ THE SISTINA CHAPEL - The Creation of the Man   THE SISTINA CHAPEL - The Creation of the Woman

Nine scenes from the Old Testament occupy the central part of this cycle of frescoes:
— **The Separation of Light and Darkness**
— **The Creation of the Sun and Moon**
— **The Separation of Land and Water**
— **The Creation of Adam**
— **The Creation of Eve**
— **The Fall and the Expulsion from Paradise**
— **The Sacrifice of Noah**
— **The Great Flood**
— **The Intoxication of Noah**

Figures of **nude Youths, Sibyls** and **Prophets** are disposed around the nine scenes. It forms a powerful majestic whole, one of the summits of Michelangelo's art.

One now goes on to the RAPHAEL STANZE, which are called after the painter who decorated them. They consist of four rooms:

Room 1: Stanza of the Borgo Fire, so called after Raphael's picture.

Room 2: Stanza della Segnatura, painted by Raphael with the allegorical figures of **Beauty, Goodness and Truth** as shown in the three famous frescoes of "Parnassus", **"The Disputation of the Sacrament"** and **"The School of Athens"**, which belong to the master's finest works.

Room 3: Stanza of Heliodorus, with another four outstanding frescoes; **"The Expulsion of Heliodorus from the Temple"**; **"The Meeting of Pope Leo I and Attila"**; **"The Miracle of Bolsena"**; **"The Deliverance of St. Peter from Prison"**.

Room 4: Stanza of Constantine: The frescoes in

THE SISTINA CHAPEL- The Deluge

this room are for the most part by Raphael's pupils.

On leaving the Raphael Stanzas, one comes to the **Loggia of Raphael** which form a magnificent Gallery with a series of vaults entirely covered with decorations. The architecture is the joint work of Bramante and Raphael; the decoration was likewise conceived by Raphael, but carried out by his pupils. The subjects are taken from the Old Testament.

Through the Loggie and then the Raphael Stanzas, one can reach the **Chapel of Pope Nicholas V**, covered with frescoes by Fra Angelico depicting **"Scenes from the Life of St. Lawrence and St. Stephen".**

The **Gallery of Maps** can also be reached through the Raphael Stanzas; it has maps of all the regions of Italy on the walls, painted by Danti.

Next comes the GALLERY OF TAPESTRIES (with the tapestries carried out after designs of Raphael and Leonardo da Vinci); THE GALLERY OF CANDELARA (containing a fine collection of Greek and Roman candelabra and copies, as well as interesting pieces of sculpture), and THE ROOM OF THE CHARIOT (so called after the fine chariot from the 1st century B.C.).

THE GREGORIAN ETRUSCAN MUSEUM and the GREGORIAN EGYPTIAN MUSEUM are the last two departments of this vast series of Museums and Galleries. They are both very interesting for their full documentation of Etruscan and Egyptian art and civilisation, and especially for certain exceptionally rare pieces in these collections.

On leaving the Museums, it is possible to visit the **Vatican Gardens**, which, though not very large, are very attractive, since they preserve the characteristic features of the fine Italian Renaissance gardens.

THE SISTINA CHAPEL
The Prophet Isaiah

THE SISTINA CHAPEL
The Prophet Daniel

THE SISTINA CHAPEL
The Prophet Zacharias

120

THE SISTINA CHAPEL
The Delphic Sibyl

THE SISTINA CHAPEL
The Cumaean Sibyl

THE SISTINA CHAPEL
Libyan Sibyl

CASTELGANDOLFO

We present now some pictures of places not far away from Rome, which may be interesting from the religious, artistic and tourist points of view. We begin from Castel Gandolfo, one of the centres of the so called «Roman Castels», at 426 metres on the sea level, which can be easily reached by train. Here the landscape is characterized by the Lake of Albano, of volcanic origin, of which we show here a fine sight, with an air-view of the Papal Villa. The importance of Castel Gandolfo is mainly due to the fact that it is the summer residence of the Pope, who spends here the warmest months of the year. The Papal Villa, has been enlarged by adding the villas Barberini and Cybo to it. In the interior there are the interesting remains of the Villa of Domitian.

The town is also a holiday resort, because of its pleasant landscape and mild climate in Summer. Many foreign tourists visit it mainly to «see the Pope» on some special occasion.

LIBERTY SQUARE AND PAPAL PALACE ➤

GARDENS AND PALACE PAPAL

GENERAL VIEW ↘

TIVOLI - VILLA D'ESTE

Tivoli, some 30 Km. from Rome, is one of the favourite and most visited tourist attractions.

The town is of very ancient origin, as shown by the archaeological remains dating from prehistoric, Etruscan and Roman times. Some of these are particularly interesting: the **Temple of Vesta** or of the **Sibyl,** a fine round building, made into the Church of Santa Maria della Rotonda in the Middle Ages; the **Temple of Tussis,** probably a tomb dating from Roman times; the **Sanctuary of Hercules,** now a vast mass of ruins.

Tivoli however has also other beauties to offer: in addition to the **Cathedral,** the **Church of San Silvestro** and other monuments, the **Villa Gregoriana** and the famous **Ville d'Este** are special attractions. **Villa Gregoriana** is a beautiful park with the famous Waterfalls of the river Anio. From the Belvedere opposite the largest waterfall one enjoys a marvellous view. In addition to this, there are other, smaller, still more picturesque falls in the Grottoes of the Sirens and of Neptune, or scattered through the park.

Villa d'Este, whose lovely **garden** is deservedly famous all over the world, merits a special visit.

It was built in the 16th century by Pirro Ligorio, and decorated by Zuccari, Tempesta and Muziano.

However the garden is its greatest glory, one of the finest examples of the so-called Italian Garden. Architecture and nature here blend to perfection, and to make the scene still more attractive, there are the many fountains and waterfalls, designed and executed in a manner as original as it is harmonious. It will suffice to mention the majestic **Fountain of the Hydraulic Organ** (where an organ, no longer working, used to paly by means of the water jets), the **Hundred Fountains,** the **Three Fishing Ponds** (three large basins connected with the Organ Fountain), and many others.

Hadrian's Villa near Tivoli, must be mentioned separately. It is one of the largest villas and one of the most interesting from the artistic point of view, The Emperor Hadrian had it built in the second century A.D.; he often liked to copy famous buildings and places of the ancient world. The following are particularly memorable: the Nymphaeum of the Island, the Stoa Poikile (painted portico), the Baths, and the Emperor's Palace, not to mention the decorations, the sculptures and the beauty of the site itself.

VILLA D'ESTE
Hundred Fountaines alley

VILLA D'ESTE ➤
The Organ's Fountain

L. 12.000
I.V.A. compresa